GOING TO

**A Doctor, a Colorado Town, and Stories from
an Unlikely Gender Crossroads**

TRINIDAD

GOING TO

**A Doctor, a Colorado Town, and Stories from
an Unlikely Gender Crossroads**

TRINIDAD

MARTIN J. SMITH

BOWER
HOUSE

DENVER

www.BowerHouseBooks.com

Designed by Margaret McCullough
Cover photography thanks to iStock

Printed in Canada

Library of Congress Control Number: 2020943997

Hardcover ISBN: 978-1-917895-10-1
Ebook ISBN: 978-1-917895-12-5

10 9 8 7 6 5 4 3 2 1

To those with the courage to be themselves

"What's that?"

—Dr. Stanley H. Biber, in 1969,
responding to a friend who had asked if he might
consider performing a delicate operation
by explaining, "I'm transsexual."

Contents

Preface—Crossroads

In deciding to pursue this story, I relied on a central truth I've always known as a journalist and as a novelist: The best stories are about people who find themselves at a crossroads. They face a critical choice, and the choice they make in that crucible moment tells us who they are. It has been my privilege while writing this book to meet many thoughtful and articulate individuals who have stood at that crossroads.

I set out to interview some of the people whose personal journeys brought them to Trinidad, Colorado, and to talk to them about their pre- and post-surgery lives, to understand their range of experiences, and to tell the stories of some remarkable people who were part of it all. I couldn't agree more with Andrea Long Chu, a writer and critic who concluded a remarkable *New York Times* essay published the week before her 2018 gender confirmation surgery with the line: "There are no good outcomes in transition. There are only people, begging to be taken seriously."

I tried to take seriously the people you'll meet in these pages—their pain, their confusion, their decisions, their triumphs, their disappointments, and their courage to find their destiny, regardless of anyone else's definition of happiness or success. To them and to all those with the courage to be themselves, I dedicate this book.

I did not set out to argue whether gender confirmation surgery is good or bad, or effective or not. My focus remained on the individuals whose stories unspool in *Going to Trinidad*. I did not choose their particular stories to advocate for any specific point of view or agenda, even if the individuals themselves do. I chose them because they struck me as endlessly compelling people who, at their personal crossroads, made a difficult choice, and in doing so committed to living with the consequences of that choice.

That includes Walt Heyer, a rare exception among the overwhelming number of Trinidad success stories, which are embodied in this book by Claudine Griggs. Walt's role in recent years as a self-styled leader of what he calls the "sex-change regret" movement has understandably made him a lightning rod for the LGBTQ community, and his story is colored by complicated personal, religious, and political views that some may find objectionable. I chose to focus on his lifelong struggle with mental illness; telling his story is not intended as an endorsement of his ideas, to offer him a platform, or to make his unusual experience seem more common than it is.

I accept that I began this journey ill-prepared and uneducated—a consequence of growing up in an era when most people believed gender was a binary thing. I'm still learning, and hope others who read this book will learn with me. I appreciate the privilege of being trusted to tell these stories.

Finally, I'm convinced of one thing with absolute certainty: This often overlooked chapter in transgender history is an effective prism through which to view a vastly more complex story that in recent years has become a long-overdue national discussion. My sincere hope is that *Going to Trinidad* will be an important part of that conversation.

1

On December 12, 1990, a law-office secretary and part-time English graduate student in Rancho Cucamonga, California, sat down to write a letter that had been nearly four decades in the making. Her name was Claudine Toni Griggs.

The diminutive Griggs had lived as a woman for sixteen years, since the summer of 1974, though she'd been born and spent the first twenty-one years of her life as Claude Anthony Griggs. So complete had been her outward transformation from male to female that few of her friends and professional colleagues suspected. Her physical stature—just five-feet-five and one-hundred-thirty pounds—gave her an advantage. "All I had to do to look sexually ambiguous was shave what little facial hair I had," she says. Plus, for seventeen years she'd been taking hormone treatments that eased her even further toward the female end of the gender spectrum. Her transition had stalled short of the next logical step, surgery to transform her male genitalia into that of a female, but by early December 1990 Griggs had made peace with that decision.

During a routine appointment with her endocrinologist less than two weeks earlier, though, her doctor had asked a direct, provocative question: "When are you planning to have surgery?"

"Never," she replied. "I've learned to live without it."

The doctor pressed. "*Why* don't you want to have the surgery?"

When she'd explored the possibility in the 1970s, Griggs told him, she'd found the attitudes of the doctors she approached off-putting. Her half-dozen encounters with various surgeons, medical centers, psychiatrists, and others left her feeling they were "less than knowledgeable, sometimes less than competent and less than ethical." In her journal, she later allowed herself to remember those difficult encounters: "If you do everything we tell you, when we tell you, and convince us you will be successful as a woman (their definition of 'success'), then we will consider, after keeping you under our scrutiny for several years, whether to authorize final sex-reassignment; and bear in mind, we rarely approve surgery (no alternative was ever mentioned). On one occasion, I met with a slightly more dangerous attitude: 'If you've got the money, I'll do surgery—immediately.'"

Once, in 1977, she'd gotten as far as scheduling the operation—only to find out the chosen surgeon lost his medical license just weeks before he was set to put her under. "I was told by another physician that 'he had butchered a couple of people,'" Griggs later recalled. "To this day, I do not believe I have completely recovered from the experience."

The endocrinologist shook his head, assuring Griggs that things had improved. And despite her anxiety about revisiting the idea, she couldn't escape that thought as she left his office that Saturday morning. A "familiar and terrible emotional storm" began to swell, and she found herself crying during the drive home. Five days later, by phone, she asked the doctor to help her identify and locate one of the specialists he'd suggested might help. The doctor referred her to a nun in nearby Orange County who he said had experience in connecting transsexuals with a doctor who could do the type of surgery she was seeking. Although they never met, Griggs today believes the nun was herself a transsexual woman and was prepared to make a referral based on personal experience.

Griggs made the call. After a phone consultation in which Griggs answered questions about how long she'd lived as a woman, whether she was taking hormones, and if she was in counseling, the nun simply said: "Most patients go to Dr. Biber."

Who?

Griggs was given contact information for an office in a place that sounded like the middle of nowhere, a small town two hundred miles south of Denver near the New Mexico border that the *New York Times* many years later would describe as "the sex-change capital of the world": Trinidad, Colorado.

"I had never heard of Dr. Biber or Trinidad until I was referred to his office, and I really didn't want to travel so far for the surgery," Griggs says. "But I wanted the procedure badly enough to do it nonetheless."

———————

Griggs's improbable advisor, the Orange County nun, was correct. Since 1969, Dr. Stanley H. Biber had been specializing in something that few surgeons dared attempt, and he had been doing so in perhaps the unlikeliest place on the planet. Trinidad, a small town along the southern Colorado-northern New Mexico border, once was a coal-mining and ranching outcrop that today is home to only about 8,000 people. While it has a colorful history and maintains a charming downtown, Trinidad has always been the kind of place where road-numbed motorists traveling Interstate 25 between Denver and Santa Fe exit just long enough to top off their gas tank, refill their go-cups, and use the bathroom. Trinidad's only hospital—serving a population that's more than fifty percent Hispanic—still has only twenty-five beds. Biber had performed the first of more than six thousand gender confirmation surgeries there in 1969 during a career that eventually would last until he was in his eighties.

The self-assured surgeon—himself a bantam at five-five, but who once was a bodybuilder—had honed his surgical skills as chief surgeon of a MASH unit during the Korean War and spent the early years of his career focused on standard appendectomies, tonsillectomies, and C-section births. But one day a social worker and personal friend asked a question at the end of an otherwise routine appointment: Would Biber consider performing a delicate surgery?

"Of course I can do your surgery. What do you want done?"

His visitor explained that she was a transsexual woman.

"What's that?" he replied.

At the time most US surgeons had heard of what then were called sex-change operations, but few had ever performed one. Only thirteen years had passed since the phrase "sex change" first entered the American lexicon when Bronx GI George

Jorgensen traveled to Denmark to become Christine Jorgensen. But Biber never lacked for confidence and began researching the idea. He consulted a doctor in New York who'd performed the male-to-female surgery, snagged some hand-drawn diagrams from Johns Hopkins, and without informing his bosses at the then Catholic hospital, agreed to give the experimental operation a try. It was the beginning of a medical specialty he never could have imagined. As he began to refine his techniques, word got around. By the time Griggs first heard his name in late 1990, the phrase "Going to Trinidad" had become a familiar euphemism for undergoing that type of surgery among transsexual men and women around the world.

Griggs thanked the nun for the information, hung up the phone, and stared for several minutes at the "precious scribbling" on her notepad. "Don't get too excited," she remembers thinking. "Don't get your hopes up until you have actually heard from this person." She knew the screening process to qualify for the surgery could be rigorous, based on guidelines recommended for treating those with gender dysphoria.[1] She also knew that only a handful of doctors in the world were capable of doing what she wanted done. It was a long shot, and she was afraid to imagine. For people like her, she later wrote, "the distance from faintish optimism to the brink of suicide can be very short."

Six days later, according to her journal, Griggs sat down at her keyboard and began to type.

"Dear Dr. Biber," she began, trying to sound businesslike and restrained. "I was referred to your office by Dr. Herbert Roberts, MD (a pseudonym Griggs created for UCLA's Dr. Gerald Leve to mask his identity, among others, in her published journal). Dr. Roberts indicates that many of his transsexual patients have had surgery through your office. I have been under Dr. Roberts's care for 17 years. Would you please send me information regarding your requirements for my having surgery through your office? If you need more information or have any questions, do not hesitate to call. Thank you, and I am looking forward to hearing from you. Very truly yours, Claudine Griggs."

She recorded her feelings about posting the letter in her journal. Reflecting on the letter's tone, she wrote: "I don't want to sound as if I'm begging, because I have determined that I will not plead my case from my knees." Of the quiet desperation that took hold once it was in the mail, she added: "I am afraid that the surgeon will respond too soon; I worry that he will not respond at all; I fear that he will die or retire before I can have the operation; I dread the surgery; I dread more a life without it."

But the holidays were fast approaching, as were her master's degree exams. During holiday meals of turkey, dressing, pie, and wine with family and friends, she idly wondered, "Will I be alive next Christmas? Will I be female?"

But for Griggs, it was all overshadowed by a question that speaks to the razor's edge walked daily by so many who struggle with gender dysphoria: Which of those alternatives would better ease the pain?

———————

Just three weeks later, Griggs found a letter in her mailbox postmarked Trinidad, Colorado, from the offices of Dr. Stanley Biber. She braced herself.

Biber's response was, she says, "a pleasant shock." His letter simply described the available services—genital surgery, breast implants, a tracheal shave to reduce the Adam's apple, rhinoplasty—and their corresponding costs. It described the need for two psychiatric evaluations recommending her for surgery, and the need to write and forward to Biber a social history of herself. Also, Griggs was told that she must have been living full-time as a woman for at least one year before she would be considered. She'd already been living openly as a woman for seventeen.

The cost breakdown, payable in full at the time of the surgery, would be as follows: Biber's surgical fee, $4,850; hospital cost, $5,435; anesthesiologist fee, $925. Breast implants were not included, but were available for an extra cost. Insurance would not cover the surgery, the letter noted, but Biber promised to refund appropriate fees if she made a successful claim against her medical insurer. It ended: "We will be glad to help if you can meet our requirements."

Again, Griggs began to cry.

By January 21, 1991, less than two months after she first wrote to Biber, Griggs was ready to post another letter that included the requested "brief social history." It was ten pages long, single-spaced, beginning with her birth as Claude in Millington, Tennessee, thirty-seven years before; her youth as the child of an Air Force and California National Guard "lifer"; her primary and secondary education in Southern California; her own year and a half as a communications specialist in the Air Force; her honorable discharge from the military after revealing her gender identity situation; her education and work history; and her generally unsatisfying sexual history with both male and female lovers. At the time, she wrote, she was involved in a four-year relationship with a woman named Carolyn, "the first relationship I have ever dared hope would be permanent."

"I have asked myself why, if I am so happy, do I seek out a surgeon as I approach middle age; I can come up with only partial answers," she explained to Biber. "I know that if surgery were impossible to attain, I could survive without it, bearing the discomfort of my present physical condition in much the same way (I think) I might bear up if I were paralyzed from the waist down and had to spend my life in a wheelchair. It would be a distressing situation, it would present some grave obstacles, it would be depressing, but it would not stop me from reaching out to work, study, learn, and just keep moving through life."

She also enclosed a photograph and noted in closing that the cost would be manageable. "I may flinch when I withdraw the funds from my savings, but I can afford your fees."

Three months later, on April 27, Griggs got the answer that both thrilled and frightened her. Biber accepted her as a "surgical candidate" and enclosed a four-page information packet called "The Trinidad Experience: Information About Your Hospital Stay (Male to Female Procedure)." But the decision was not yet final, Biber explained: "Though you have been accepted as a *candidate*, please bear in mind that I will make the final decision in my office the day prior to your scheduled surgery."

Still, Griggs allowed herself some hope. Fifteen years after her first attempts to find a surgeon, she found herself reassured by this voice from the Colorado wilderness, by Biber's professionalism and confidence, by the fact that "medical care is being offered almost routinely to a subdued transsexual who had given up looking for a remedy, resolving instead to accept the pain of existence—physically, legally, psychologically—in a kind of sexual limbo."

For the first time in what seemed like forever, Claudine Griggs imagined the life she felt born to live.

2

Walt Heyer's journey to Trinidad—his first one, anyway, the one that ended in panic, uncertainty, a hasty return bus trip to Denver, and a flight back to his home in Southern California—actually began in San Francisco's Tenderloin District, in a bar called The Roadrunner.

How he got there, dressed as a woman, is a complicated story. Actually, the word "complicated" doesn't really describe the tortured road of sexual torment and confusion, mental illness, alcohol and drug abuse, secrecy, deceit, and self-loathing that Heyer had traveled to that point in his life. He was forty-one years old, a husband and father, working as the national manager of port operations for American Honda Motor Company, an enormous job with enormous responsibility for overseeing the arrival of cargo ships full of cars from Japan and distributing them via trains and trucks to dealerships across the country. This was in 1981, and the Honda brand was just starting to take off in the US. Heyer was married sixteen years, and his work required him to travel almost daily to ports in California, New Jersey, Virginia, Florida, Texas, Illinois, Oregon, Hawaii, and Puerto Rico. Still, when working in the port of Richmond, near San Francisco, he made time to be himself, or at least the version of himself he sincerely believed he was meant to be.

The woman sitting at The Roadrunner was the same woman Heyer had suspected had been inside him for decades, ever since his maternal grandmother, an expert seamstress he called Mamy, began taking her four-year-old grandson into her walk-in closet and secretly dressing him in girl's clothing. She eventually sewed him a purple chiffon full-length evening dress. As much as he enjoyed those play sessions with her at the time, looking back years later he recalls that purple dress as "the most destructive force in my life."

Why did she do it? "I think she just got excited about it," Heyer says of his late grandmother. "But that purple chiffon dress, that was pretty much a commitment on her part. I have no idea why. That was her deal, and I can't speak to why she did it or what motivated her. She just did it. I don't think she had a clue."

That purple dress led, eventually, to a painful confrontation with his strict parents, and to a pivot point in his relationship with the father he adored. "Without any malice intended on her part, Grandma Mamy, with her gift of a purple dress, unwittingly set the table not only for my next painful and disturbing experience, but for a lifelong struggle with my identity as a man."

For more than three decades before that evening in The Roadrunner, Heyer had sensed the presence of a force he did not understand, this "girl who lived in my head." She first identified herself as Christal West. He says she grew up with him, "demanding more and more of my time." He began cross-dressing more often, in secret, an obsession he compares to feeding a small fire that just gets bigger and bigger, a battle that went on "all day, every day."

Later, this girl who "nagged me about having a life of her own" convinced him in the mid-1970s to start taking female hormones under the supervision of an "underground" Beverly Hills doctor. Those hormones seemed to make her more powerful, and she eventually started calling herself Andrea West. She's the one who convinced him to get the first of many cosmetic surgeries, a tummy tuck to hide the stomach sag left behind after he'd lost weight. The indisputable facts of his life were those of a stable family man, a hard-drinking workaholic executive, the faithful son raised by parents he loved despite their intolerance of his grandmother's doting indulgences. Less obvious was the constant inner turmoil he'd shared with no one.

"How did she get inside me?" Heyer reflected years later. "How could she have so much control and power to destroy me?"

When he was fourteen, he heard the story of George William Jorgensen, Jr., a former GI who in 1951 had traveled from his Bronx home to Copenhagen, Denmark, to undergo a series of operations that physically transformed him into a woman.

Jorgensen returned from Europe as Christine Jorgensen, and thanks to a sensational front-page story in the *New York Daily News*, became America's first transgender celebrity.[2]

"That's the first time I heard it was possible," he says now. "When you're struggling with issues like I did, you're looking for a model and example that shows you can do it. Those tend to spark people into thinking, 'Now that's who I am!' So during that time, Christine Jorgensen was my model."

Heyer remembers feeling at that moment like he was filled with gasoline as a match was struck. "I wanted to do that. Knowing the change from a man to a woman was possible gave me new hope. I could fantasize about a new life, free from the past. This fantasizing, over time, became an obsession."

Heyer was good at keeping his secret, though, and that obsession never impeded his career. After relocating his family from Southern California to Sonoma, just north of San Francisco, Heyer found himself making excuses to visit the seedy, fifty-square-block area of San Francisco known as the Tenderloin, an area that has stubbornly resisted gentrification for decades and which remains popular with gay men and women, transvestites, drug dealers, and prostitutes. The arrest of a drag queen at Compton's Cafeteria there in 1966 triggered a riot that predated by three years the more famous gay uprising at New York's Stonewall Inn.

At first, Heyer says he just drove through the area. Soon he was stepping out of his car and going into bars, meeting people, making friends. The encounters were not sexual, he insists. "That's not untypical," he says. "Many transgender people are not homosexual. Many are asexual."

Eventually, using a new friend's nearby apartment to change into women's clothing, he began visiting the Tenderloin bars as a woman. Then, after removing his clothes and makeup and changing back into business attire, he'd return home to his family. "At the peak of [business] success, I was also at the peak of my desire to undergo gender reassignment surgery."

Until then, his was a self-diagnosis. But still, it felt like an answer to the questions that had confounded him for years.

That night, as luck would have it, a transvestite he'd met at The Roadrunner knew just enough about the subject to lead Heyer to what he considered the next logical step—a doctor who could prescribe female hormones. But the experiment was unsatisfying, he recalls: "The hormones didn't seem to do much, other than have a slight tranquilizing effect and lower my libido."

He wanted more. Telling his wife he was headed to Lake Tahoe to visit a car dealership, Heyer eventually booked an appointment with a plastic surgeon who implanted what he describes as "large breasts, about forty-twos or something." Hiding them from his business colleagues during the day was simply a matter of mashing them down beneath a wide strip of elastic. Hiding them from his wife was another matter. She'd known about his cross-dressing since before they were married, and always had been understanding and tolerant. But breasts? No. That was too much. At that point, Heyer says, their marriage endured, but their sex life was over.

"Obviously, she was done at that point, and I understood that," he says. "I totally expected that to be the case."

Through other contacts he'd made at The Roadrunner, Heyer arranged a meeting with psychologist Paul Walker. At the time, Walker was the go-to guy in the Bay Area for people struggling with sexual identity issues. He'd started his private practice just a year before Heyer found him and specialized in treating patients with gender dysphoria. Heyer considered their meeting an initial step toward an even more radical surgery than breast implantation—the surgery about which he'd fantasized for so long.

Even then, many psychologists understood the delicacy of such decisions, and most required male patients seeking the surgery to live as a woman for at least twelve months before undergoing the operation. In fact, Walker had helped create those standards, which applied equally to women who wanted to surgically become men, in a process now commonly called "transitioning." Heyer and Walker chitchatted a bit, and Walker asked Heyer to tell him his life story in short form. He dutifully covered the formative chapters of his life, including his grandmother's dress-up sessions, an episode when a teenaged uncle sexually molested him at age ten, and his family's steadfast refusal to take his word over the denials of the uncle. His mother, he recalls, accused him of lying.

Walker listened, and at the end of the hour-long session told his new patient that he suspected Heyer suffered from gender dysphoria, and that the proper therapy for him was a regimen of female hormones, followed by surgery.

"He was convinced after an hour," Heyer now recalls. "I wasn't, but he was."

The following week, after another hour-long session, Walker made an official diagnosis. At the start of their third session, Heyer says Walker gave him a letter recommending him for the operation.

"And so it came to be in 1981 I decided to end the lifetime of waiting and do the one thing I believed would make my mental anguish go away," Heyer wrote years later.

By then, between his public drinking and private cross-dressing, lying came easily to the forty-two-year-old. He booked a flight to Denver and a Greyhound ticket for the five-hour bus trip from there to Trinidad. He told his family he was going on a business trip and told his employer he was taking a vacation. What he was really planning was to have the renowned Dr. Stanley Biber of Trinidad, Colorado, remove his penis and testicles and handcraft a new vagina, all without telling his wife. Or anyone.

The choice of Biber was simple, Heyer recalls. "He was the only one anyone talked about. At the time he was the only one doing the surgery. I had tried to get into UCLA and other places, but everyone had shut down their clinics. There was nothing left. You had one choice."

———————

A taxi dropped him at Biber's office in Trinidad's First National Bank, the five-story sandstone landmark at Main and Commercial in the historic heart of Trinidad. The stocky doctor who greeted him for their first in-person consultation was a curious presence.

The short, avuncular surgeon, a former weightlifter, looked a bit like a cannonball with glasses. Recollections of first encounters with Biber often are quite similar. Recalling their first meeting, for example, Claudine Griggs described the surgeon as "just enough overweight to remind me of Marlon Brando in *The Godfather*," but "as gentle and kind as a fictional country doctor dedicatedly making his rounds through all weather and adversity." He reminded her of Dr. Burleigh in Willa Cather's story "Neighbour Rosicky," with his "natural good manners."

But Biber's office, Heyer remembers, was less inviting. "It was above the old bank, like something out of an old movie set version of a psychiatric hospital," he said. "It was old, run down. It was much more scary than it was impressive. I'm guessing this is what people felt like when they were going to an abortion clinic."

Biber was friendly as he greeted Heyer, but focused on the business at hand. He asked Heyer to review his personal history and studied the surgical recommendation from Walker. After Biber agreed to do the surgery, Heyer handed over a check for the $7,500 surgeon's fee and agreed to pay the additional hospital fees. Did Heyer like Biber? "I just looked at him as a person who had the skill to do this surgery," Heyer says. "That was more important than liking him."

Heyer took a taxi from Biber's office to Mt. San Rafael, the hospital where Biber had scheduled him for surgery the following day. He underwent some blood work and pre-paid the remaining hospital costs.

"I remember feeling like I was in a dream that I couldn't wake up from, a dream that I had no power to stop, although I wanted to," Heyer remembers. "Walking into the hospital after the cab ride, I started getting a very sick feeling. ... At this moment, in this hospital, in this waiting room, I had never felt more alone, more twisted or powerless."

He rose from his chair and started walking Trinidad's streets, crying, his head awash with questions. He thought about his wife and two children. How could he do this to them? How could he do this to his body? Was surgery the only way to solve his problem? After an hour, he was back at Biber's office, telling the surgeon he'd decided to forego the scheduled operation. Biber, unflappable by all accounts, seemed nonplussed. The doctor returned half of his fee and told Heyer he'd be happy to perform the operation later if Heyer changed his mind.

Most approved surgeries proceeded as planned, and last-minute reconsiderations were uncommon among Biber's patients at Mt. San Rafael. But from time to time, a patient like Heyer would back out. Bucky Carr, who worked as Biber's nurse anesthetist for a decade between 1993 and 2003, remembers visiting one patient the night before her surgery.

"The more I talked to her, the more I was struck that she didn't seem like other transsexual patents," Carr says. "Most of the hospital rooms are semiprivate, and when we had multiple cases during the week, we put the transgender patients in rooms together. So when I bid her farewell for the evening, I passed by her roommate who'd already had her surgery. The roommate was giving me the thumbs-down and mouthing the words *She's not a transsexual!*"

Carr caught Biber on his way into the hospital the following morning, and told the surgeon about his concerns, and about what he'd seen the night before. Biber made a point to visit the patient, and at the end of their discussion the patient opted out of the surgery. Turns out, the therapist who'd approved her for the operation had no experience in dealing with transsexual men or women. Carr said he and Biber occasionally relied on their instincts in such matters.

Heyer recalls the moment he told Biber he'd changed his mind. "It was almost like he might have expected it to happen," he says. "It was very, 'OK, that's fine.' Like returning a shirt that didn't fit." Heyer got back on the bus to Denver, then a plane back home. He resolved to confess everything to his wife, already knowing it would mean the end of their nineteen-year marriage.

Their daughter was sixteen at the time; Heyer avoided telling her the truth about his personal torment by explaining that he no longer loved her mother. It was devastating for her, but it just seemed easier. Their son was twelve and reacted with more confusion than anger. Both kids eventually learned the truth. After the divorce was finalized the following year, during an agreed-upon visit with his son, Heyer remembers the boy looking up from his lunch. "I wish you had cancer," he told his father. "At least then I could tell people what was wrong with you."

Heyer bottomed out—not for the first or last time—about a year later. By then, he was reconsidering surgery. He traveled again to Trinidad under the name Walt Heyer. But when he signed the authorization papers for his operation, he signed them using the distinctive scribble of Andrea West.

3

Going to Trinidad

Not all roads led to Trinidad between 1969 and 2010, but for forty-one years in the worldwide transgender community, a startling number of them did. By the time both Walt Heyer returned to Stanley Biber's office in 1983, and Claudine Griggs showed up in 1991, the phrase "Going to Trinidad" already was well-understood shorthand among transgender men and women, easier than saying, "I've made the most difficult decision of my life," and certainly easier than trying to explain the pain, self-loathing, and emotional and psychological uncertainty that brought someone to the side entrance of the First National Bank building, up the creaking, archaic elevator or the steep stairs, to Dr. Stanley Biber's fourth-floor office for a pre-surgery consultation. "Going to Trinidad" covered it, and for those who understood, a simple nod of the head was the only response required.

Trinidad's role in transgender history has been well known in Colorado for decades. Pueblo native and Colorado historian Tim Nicklas recalls talk of Trinidad during his middle- and high-school days, the invocation of its name a convenient insult to a classmate's manhood. Bucky Carr of Boulder, Biber's nurse anesthetist at Mt. San Rafael Hospital for a decade, also remembers hearing Trinidad used as a handy taunt, a running joke for snarky Coloradans. "High school boys would say, 'If you're going to whine and cry like a girl why not go to Trinidad and become one?'" he recalls.

But outside of the state, even today among the estimated 1.4 million transgender men and women in the US, the role Trinidad played in the gender-identity universe remains, to most, an improbable surprise. It's not exactly clear why, and those who do know about it likely are part of the LGBTQ community. *The Denver Post*'s magazine told the Trinidad story in a July 1983 cover story titled "Starting Over." Writer John Tayman chronicled Biber and Trinidad in a December 1991 *Gentlemen's Quarterly* story titled "Meet John, er, Jane Doe," and Tayman accompanied one surgical pilgrim he called "Dean Wakeman" before, during, and after his operation.[3] By the mid-1990s, Biber's work was making headlines in other distant and significant publications, so it's not that word wasn't getting out. The *Los Angeles Times* featured Biber in a 1995 story by Michael Haederle headlined "The Body Builder," noting in a secondary headline that Biber had already been "correcting nature's miscues" for twenty-five years. An operating room photo accompanying that story showed Biber's face masked by surgical garb as he peered into the artfully cloaked undercarriage of an anesthetized patient, and included comments from a Biber patient named Henryetta, a twenty-two-year Army veteran who retired from the military as sergeant first-class. *Out* magazine's story that same year, by Elizabeth Cohen, told a similar tale beneath the headline "Biberpeople." It featured a different photo of Biber in surgical scrubs, but also one with the surgeon wearing his trademark Western shirt and cowboy hat and standing outside the bank building where his professional offices were housed.

Biber was even name-checked and featured in a March 9, 2005, episode of the animated television series *South Park* called "Mr. Garrison's Fancy New Vagina," in which the transgender schoolteacher character travels to see "Dr. Biber" at the "Trinidad Medical Center" to undergo the surgery.[4]

Despite the occasional spotlight stories and pop culture acknowledgments, Trinidad as "sex-change capital of the world" didn't seem to register much in the American consciousness during those years, and was easy to dismiss as a distant, somewhat sensational signal emanating from the middle of nowhere. Transgender people were the ultimate "other"—unfamiliar, a little scary, hard to fathom. But day in and day out, week after week, month after month, year after year, the pilgrims came. In addition to other surgical duties, Biber and his eventual successor, Dr. Marci Bowers, often were doing three or more gender confirmation surgeries per week. And what happened in

Trinidad didn't stay in Trinidad. Their patients invariably returned home to lives, communities, and careers, many becoming emissaries for an idea that to some still seems foreign and freakish. The Trinidad pilgrims began colonizing schools, offices, and churches, bringing with them the uncomfortable fact that transgender men and women are people with joys, sorrows, ambitions, and goals that aren't much different from anyone else's. When the "other" is your cousin, or friend, or coworker, they're damned hard to demonize.

Not that some didn't try. Local religious leaders and some politicians had moral qualms about Biber's transgender work, and their rumbling outrage was kept in check during the early years mostly by Biber's proactive approach, first with Mt. San Rafael's administrators (he kept the medical charts for his early transgender patients in the administrator's safe), and later with concerned—or at least curious—clergy and community leaders, whom he gathered for a series of lectures during which he earnestly explained his compassion toward those patients and his ability to help surgically relieve their suffering. He told one interviewer in 1998 that those local lectures were "one of the smartest things I've ever done." The locals may not have embraced the strangers who regularly arrived in Trinidad, but they accepted them.

Outside of Trinidad, the culture war raged on. By the early 1990s, as Biber continued doing his gender surgeries at Mt. San Rafael, a bitter war against the "others" had erupted just two hours to the north, in Colorado Springs. Labeled as the "Vatican of evangelical Christianity" by *US News & World Report* and the home of James Dobson's vehemently anti-gay Focus on the Family organization, that city of about 300,000 at the time also was the epicenter of efforts to further demonize sexual nonconformists by the unrelated group Colorado for Family Values. In 1992, that group spearheaded a drive to pass Amendment 2, a challenge to efforts by the state's Human Relations Commission to protect gay citizens from discrimination. A smooth-talking conservative car dealer named Wilfred Perkins fronted a statewide campaign of intense fear-mongering about a supposedly nefarious gay agenda, with one leaflet attributing the motto "Sex by eight, or it's too late" to the North American Man/Boy Love Association, and urging Coloradans to "vote yes on Amendment 2 for the future of our children."

On November 3, 1992, Colorado voters passed Amendment 2, which amended the state constitution to exclude gays from basic civil rights protections. Then Governor Roy Romer challenged the amendment, which set the stage for what Lillian Faderman, author of the encyclopedic 2015 book *The Gay Revolution*, called "the mother of anti-gay battles." The battle eventually reached the US Supreme Court, which in 1996 delivered a landmark smackdown in *Romer v. Evans*. Writing for the 6–3 majority, Justice Anthony Kennedy concluded: "A state cannot deem a class of persons a stranger to its laws."

Still, the culture war continued. Three years later, on July 4, 1999, members of the Westboro Baptist Church came to Trinidad. The unaffiliated Kansas-based church known for its incendiary rhetoric against gays arrived to picket what its news release for the event described as "Satan's physician" and the town it called the "anteroom to Hell."

––––––––––

Trinidad's history is itself a story of arduous journeys and difficult transitions. While today it may be a convenient stop for road-numbed motorists traveling Interstate 25 between Denver and Santa Fe, the city's past is inseparable from its history as a migratory pathway for dinosaurs during its pre-history, and more recently as a thoroughfare for travelers along the so-called Mountain Branch of the Santa Fe Trail settlement route into New Mexico.

Sitting at the base of a spur of the Rocky Mountains, Trinidad represents the Colorado side of Raton Pass, a 7,834-foot saddle that channels traffic between Trinidad and Raton, New Mexico, about a hundred miles northeast of Santa Fe.

One of the city's founders was Felipe de Jesus Baca, who in 1860 rode north along the Santa Fe Trail from Mora Valley, New

Mexico, to sell a load of grain at Cherry Creek. The already prosperous businessman immediately was struck by the fertile bottomland along the Purgatoire River,[5] and in the ensuing years convinced a dozen or so families from New Mexico to follow him north. According to an account in *Colorado Magazine*, their convoy of twenty ox-pulled wagons included not only families, but horses, sheep, goats, and pigs. When the slow-footed pigs hindered their progress as they struggled up and over Raton Pass, the practical Baca told his fellow travelers: "Go ahead and give those tired fellows a blow on the head, and we will eat them, and why not." They and others began laying out the town of Trinidad in 1861. In 1999, the Colorado Historical Society honored Baca as one of the fifty most influential Coloradans of all time, and he is featured prominently in the ceramic mural that greets visitors to Mt. San Rafael Hospital. Even today, the state's most southeastern county bears Baca's name. Baca House, his two-story adobe landmark home on Trinidad's Main Street, part of the legendary Santa Fe Trail, now houses a portion of the Trinidad History Museum, along with its younger brick neighbor, Bloom Mansion, and one other building.

According to a town history published in an 1871 directory of Trinidad's residents and businesses, the city was promoting the "inexhaustible beds of coal" beneath the settlement, with outcrops of that black gold visible in surrounding ravines. It also noted, "Copper and iron ores have been discovered in the vicinity, and a proper development of the mineral resources of the mountains contiguous would doubtless insure rich returns to the enterprising capitalists, and the adjacent plain to the eastward, covered with nutritious grasses, affords excellent pasturage for cattle and sheep, a source of no inconsiderable profit to persons engaged in the stock business."

According to that 1871 account, Trinidad's population of a thousand residents traded in forty stores and shops. The town also was home to a weekly newspaper, the *Trinidad Enterprise,* and the United States Hotel, "the principal and most popular public house in southern Colorado" and "a credit to the town." Trinidad even boasted its own physician and surgeon, Dr.

Michael Beshoar, after whom the city's refurbished Dr. Beshoar Building is still known today. He died in 1907 at age seventy-four, but the early prominence of a surgeon in the small community foreshadowed by half a century that of Stanley Biber.

The directory also includes an account of how the local land was wrested from the Ute tribe of Native Americans who'd lived there for generations. That one-sided, misguided historical record underscores Winston Churchill's assertion that "history is written by the victors." Trinidad's white and Mexican settlers had built the town's prosperity and promise on land wrested from those indigenous people, and therefore any unpleasantness about that transition was reduced to recaps like the one about a particularly violent episode, "kindly furnished" to the publisher of the Trinidad Directory by George S. Simpson, one of southern Colorado's earliest white settlers. Simpson is buried on a bluff overlooking the town. It's called Simpson's Rest, and today it's marked by a sometimes graffiti-scarred monument beside an illuminated Hollywood-style "T-R-I-N-I-D-A-D" sign.

As reported by Simpson: "In October 1866, the citizens of Trinidad and Las Animas County suffered all manner of indignities at the hands of the Ute Indians, under the leadership of the notorious chief, Ka-ni-ha-che. These pestiferous nomads, troublesome alike in peace and war, had hatched up some imaginary grievances, and forthwith betook themselves to the warpath. Many exposed and helpless settlers were pounced upon and murdered, their homes despoiled, and their cattle and horses driven away. So little resistance was offered that the savages became more and more violent, practicing their depredations with impunity, and threatening to depopulate the entire region."

Enter the US Cavalry. A federal troop from short-lived Fort Stevens on the Apishapa River, near Aquilar, under the command of a "Col. Alexander," arrived from about twenty miles away to sort things out. Peace talks faltered quickly, Simpson explained, so "failing all reasonable endeavors to pacify the blood-thirsty thieves, Col. Alexander abandoned Quaker arguments and appealed to the sabres and Sharpe's carbines of his men. He gave the band a terrible thrashing, killing many braves, and driving the balance out of the country. In their return, true to their instincts, they murdered and pillaged indiscriminately, but from that day the settlements in southern Colorado have been secure from the depredations of marauding red-skins."[6]

Bat Masterson was Trinidad's first marshal in the 1880s— the local La Quinta Inn at one point offered a "Bat Masterson" that includes roast beef, cheddar cheese, capers, pickles, lettuce, and tomato for $8.95—and Wyatt Earp drove the stagecoach between Trinidad and Box Springs, New Mexico. Kit Carson earned much of his reputation as a Western swashbuckler and Indian fighter during incidents that happened in and around Trinidad, which since 1910 has had a park in Carson's name at the corner of Kansas Avenue and San Pedro Street featuring a cast bronze statue of Carson on horseback. Recounting the history of Trinidad's once-luxurious three-story Columbian hotel overlooking the same intersection of Commercial and Main as Biber's private office, *GQ* writer Tayman listed its most famous visitors, including President Herbert Hoover and actor Douglas Fairbanks, Sr. "The actor Tom Mix took room 214; his horse, Tony, slept in 212. Will Rogers settled in for an evening, leaving the next day for Alaska, where he died in a plane crash."

———————

By 1910, America was running on coal. Given as a birthday present from John D. Rockefeller to his namesake son, Colorado Fuel & Iron Company operated the largest steel mills in the West, as well as dozens of mines, coke ovens, transportation lines, and other infrastructure needed to support the industry. As the largest private employer and the largest landowner in the state, CF&I created countless small communities for the mine workers it recruited from throughout Europe, operating on the presumption that people who spoke different languages were less likely to recognize their common interests and organize into labor unions to improve their often brutal working conditions. The remains of their lives dot the landscape around Trinidad today, from the hive-like coke ovens in Cokedale about seven miles outside of town, to the preserved company medical offices at the Steelworks Museum in Pueblo.

But by 1913, a half century of worker discontent over safety and wages came to a head in a strike that early the following year brought fabled labor activist Mary "Mother" Jones, by then eighty-two years old, to Trinidad and nearby coal fields and ultimately landed her in jail. Miners were evicted from their company houses, so the United Mine Workers set up a series of tent camps where the striking miners could live. With a restricted supply of coal, steel production began to lag. Simmering tensions exploded in the spring of 1914.

By then, the Colorado National Guard units that at first had been deployed to keep the peace had been replaced by troops that often were employees of the mine company wearing guard uniforms. Their mission became less about keeping the peace than about protecting the interests of the mine owners, a fact which became more and more obvious as the spring went on. They engaged in a terror campaign against the striking workers, driving through the tent cities in a CF&I-built armored vehicle with a mounted machine gun, spraying fire over the heads of the strikers.

On April 20 that year, national guardsmen beat and shot to death one of the strike's most respected leaders, Louis Tikas, who had approached the guardsmen to try and ease the tension. A day-long battle between enraged strikers and the guardsman followed quickly in the Ludlow encampment. Eleven children and two women were caught in their hiding places beneath the tents, their deaths providing the greatest outrage of the day and drawing coverage from national news organizations. For ten days after what's now known as the Ludlow Massacre, miners engaged in a pitched battle against those they perceived as their tormentors, becoming what Colorado state historian William J. Convery has called "the bloodiest civil insurrection in American history since the Civil War." It ended only after President Woodrow Wilson dispatched federal troops to quell the violence, but what happened in Ludlow became a touchstone for labor organizers around the country.

The coal industry began to fade in the 1920s, and was pretty much gone by the 1970s. But Trinidad transformed again, achieving a strange sort of prosperity, or at least notoriety, during Prohibition when Chicago mobster Al Capone and his family hid out in Trinidad and nearby Aguilar by blending in with the Italian immigrant families who continued to call the city home. During that period, according to a 2016 account in the Trinidad-based *New Legends Magazine*, the tunnels beneath the city were said to provide safe passage for local traffic in bootleg booze. Later, in the 1940s, the magazine claims the FBI linked Joe Bonanno, the infamous leader of New York's "five families," to the Trinidad-based Colorado Cheese Company, which allegedly was among a network of twenty-three cheese and pizza companies affiliated with organized crime.[7]

Those bursts of prosperity had left Trinidad with a number of lavish hotels, a Carnegie Library, an opera house, churches, and the oldest continuously active synagogue in the state. A promotional film posted to YouTube in 2012 by the Colorado Department of Transportation referred to Trinidad as "the Victorian jewel of southern Colorado" without ever once mentioning the medical claim to fame for which today it is best known. When *Out* magazine sent writer Elizabeth Cohen there in 1995, though, Trinidad was what Cohen called "a very bad locale even to hold hands with someone of the same gender." Main Street, at the time, "consists of the Safeway, some dreary-looking bars with cheesy western names like The Alamo and The Lone Star, McLaren's Office Products, Skateland, and the dark sockets of many empty storefronts. The Trinidad Opera House, obviously a very grand place when it was built in 1882, today stands empty and boarded up, as does the once elegant Columbian Hotel."

What remains of the city's mining history is found today in monuments commemorating the triumphs and tragedies of that era, from the Ludlow Tent Colony Site memorial a few miles north of town, to the strange downtown Coal Miner's

Canary Memorial (a giant bronze canary in a cage) dedicated in 2010 to acknowledge the yellow songbird that "has saved countless human lives" as an early indicator of danger in the mines, to the adjacent 1997 Southern Colorado Coal Miners Memorial, the walkway to which is paved with the bricks once made in a factory just outside of town. Each brick proudly bears the stamp "Trinidad."

It's hard to overstate the impact that the Cincinnati-based Sisters of Charity had on Trinidad. In 1868, prosperous pioneer Felipe Baca donated land for the order to create a Catholic school in the middle of town. The sisters arrived in 1870 and set up the school, doing such a good job that the county school board asked them to also operate the town's public school. Thus began Colorado's first school district, operating out of a two-story adobe school adjacent to the 1885 Holy Trinity Catholic Church. It operated as the Sister's Academy until 1892.

The original Mt. San Rafael Hospital, with its elegant stained-glass windows, also was built by the Cincinnati-based Sisters of Charity in 1889 and run by that Catholic religious order for the next eighty years. The order turned control of the hospital over to the Trinidad Area Health Association in the early 1970s, not long after Stanley Biber did his first gender confirmation surgery there, but stayed involved with the hospital for decades afterward. The last Sister of Charity affiliated with the hospital died in 1993.

In 1976, the Trinidad Area Health Association commissioned Sister Augusta Zimmer to create a mosaic for the lobby of the new hospital building it built on the site to replace the original. By then, the nun was a well-known artist and former chair of the art department at Mount St. Joseph College in Cincinnati, the order's home base which has been known since 2014 as Mount St. Joseph University, but known colloquially and somewhat inappropriately as "the Mount" or "Old Mount." The health association envisioned something grand that would capture the strength and beauty of the landscape as well as the colorful history of the wild west city.

Sister Augusta weighed her options, and eventually recommended a multifaceted mosaic made entirely of ceramic. Having talked her distant patrons into that unusual approach, she then had some tough choices to make. Which facets of Trinidad's long and colorful history to leave in, and which to leave out? She had 336 square feet to work with in the envisioned twenty-eight-by-twelve-foot space, and her choices say a lot about Trinidad's uneasy relationship with what eventually became its medical claim to fame.

Bat Masterson didn't make the cut. Nor did Mary "Mother" Jones, or Al Capone. Sister Augusta also left out the long history of Utes despite beginning her historical timeline with the arrival of the Spanish conquistadores in the late 1500s. Their quest for the fabled Seven Cities of Gold is depicted in the work's upper left corner, showing them gathered on the banks of the Purgatoire.

The Ohio-based nun plunged into historical research and got to know the landscape surrounding Trinidad. She acknowledged its rough beauty in a collage that runs across the top of the mural, showing the Sangre de Cristo (Blood of Christ) mountain range west of the city, including the majestic twin Spanish Peaks and Fishers Peak, the distinctive flattop tower that looms over the town like a cartoon mountain that's been horizontally scissored in half. She created a ceramic facsimile of the Ludlow Monument that commemorates the famous 1914 labor massacre, another commemorating Trinidad's first school, and others showing transportation from different eras, including stagecoaches, an Amtrak train, and a tractor-trailer. Even the Trinidad High School gym, built in 1972, topped with a distinctive gold geodesic roof and home of the Mighty Miners, got a panel. So did the original hospital building and the peculiar Ave Maria shrine that overlooks it from a hillside across the hospital parking lot.

That shrine may embody Trinidad's deeply Catholic heritage more than anything else in town. According to an account written by the Catholic Diocese of Pueblo, which now owns it, the shrine is the result of a somewhat creepy and mystifying event in 1908. As the local legend goes, a Trinidad physician, Dr. John Espy, was leaving the hospital after all-night duty. It was barely dawn and snowing hard, but he was determined to make it home. As he was leaving, he noticed a light flickering on the hill directly behind the hospital. Was he snow blind? Or might someone be hurt or stranded? Despite the weather and his end-of-shift exhaustion, Espy decided to investigate. He struggled up the frozen hillside toward the light, and in a small clearing he found a 250-pound statue of the Virgin Mary with a lit candle flickering at its base. How did it get there, and why was the candle still lit in the storm's cutting winds? He called out to see if someone was nearby, but got no answer. He remained with the statue until after daybreak, the candle still flickering, and still no one came.

The diocese now qualifies that story rather bluntly: "We do not know if this story is true or not."

Still, word got around. The true believers declared the discovery a divine sign. They decided back then that a shrine should be built on that spot in the Virgin's honor. The early settlers erected a small lava rock grotto and placed the statue inside. For years they made daily pilgrimages and offered prayers for the Virgin's intercession. Plans for a more elaborate shrine were launched in 1934, propelled by the devotion of a group of local Catholics devoted to Mary known as the Circolo Mariano. That structure is the one that exists today. But in 1962, vandals destroyed the statue, breaking it into what the diocese rather precisely describes as "279 pieces." A local craftsman restored the statue, and it was moved inside and placed above the altar, where it remains today—albeit under heavy padlock. The shrine is unlocked by appointment only.

The veracity of that story notwithstanding, Sister Augusta decided to include a small version of the shrine in her mural. She also reserved a half-moon-shaped panel in the middle left to spotlight three specific Trinidad "pioneers"—the only three individuals she accorded star treatment. One of those three is Dr.

Michael Beshoar, Trinidad's first physician, whom the brochure credits with organizing, guiding, informing, and furthering "the cultural, intellectual, and political life of the community." The other two pioneers are Don Felipe Baca and Frank G. Bloom, a key player in building the coal industry in the region.

Four panels in the mural acknowledge Trinidad's most prominent religious structures, including downtown's Holy Trinity Catholic Church, the Zion Lutheran Church, the Methodist Church, and Temple Aaron, the 1889 Victoria-Moorish synagogue that's the oldest in Colorado and where Biber, a former rabbinical student, sometimes led services when a rabbi was unavailable.

The finished ceramic mural took four years to create and weighs three thousand pounds—so much that Sister Augusta asked the hospital's architect for blueprints of the two-story lobby wall to make sure it would support the ceramic beast. After realizing the envisioned plaster edifice would likely collapse under the weight, the architect amended the plans and reinforced the wall. The mural was dedicated on October 14, 1980, eleven years after Stanley Biber began making Trinidad a worldwide medical mecca by specializing in gender confirmation surgery at the hospital.

For whatever reason, Sister Augusta chose to leave out that part of Trinidad's history.

Acknowledged or not—and Stanley H. Biber is mostly not—the short, balding surgeon who arrived in Trinidad in 1954 eventually would emerge as Trinidad's best-known modern figure. With a fondness for Stetson hats, jeans, and cowboy boots, the Iowa native immediately began to sink deep roots into the place with which his name, in some circles, eventually would become synonymous.

4

Cowboy with a Scalpel

Some argue that the story of Stanley Biber in Trinidad began during a childhood train trip from his native Des Moines, Iowa, to visit an uncle who lived on a Texas ranch. That's where, according to his widow, Mary Lee, the dream of owning a ranch and running cattle may have caught fire in the young man, a dream stoked and nurtured by Biber's fondness for John Wayne movies and the Hollywood version of Old West mythology.

Another argument suggests it began more directly in Korea, during Biber's time as a battlefield surgeon in a Mobile Army Surgical Hospital, or MASH, unit. That's where he honed his skills as a surgeon while trying to save soldiers who'd been shot or who had stepped on a land mine, leaving their bodies devastated by wounds to reproductive organs, bowels, and urinary tracts. That's where he developed a reputation as tireless and determined, where he supposedly cemented his legend by performing thirty-seven consecutive surgeries before passing out, and earned a commendation for completing an operation even after shrapnel from an explosion outside the surgical unit lodged in his butt, sending a stream of his own blood down his leg as he worked.

And of course, there was a bit of serendipity involved as well.

Biber was born May 4, 1923, in Des Moines, where his father owned a furniture store and his mother stayed busy with local social causes. After briefly considering a career as a concert pianist, he graduated from high school at age sixteen and enrolled in a yeshiva in Chicago, intending to become a rabbi. As happened with so many of his generation, World War II interrupted his studies.

The basic origin story of Biber's life in Trinidad holds that he arrived in 1954 after serving as a civilian employee with the Office of Strategic Services (the forerunner of the Central

Intelligence Agency) in Alaska and the Northwest Territory during World War II. Biber, then less than twenty years old, didn't talk much about his work during that period. "Just say I was there," he told an interviewer in 1998. But Kelly Tucker, who in 1983 became Biber's financial advisor, says Biber once alluded vaguely to "blowing up Japanese radar bases."

The specific details of Biber's OSS service may be lost to history. At best, they're buried in inaccessible government records that even my Freedom of Information Act request could not excavate. But it's worth noting that in June 1942, six months after the attack on Pearl Harbor, Japanese troops invaded two remote, sparsely inhabited Aleutian islands named Attu and Kiska in what was then the American territory of Alaska. What followed is a nearly forgotten chapter of the war called the "Aleutian Islands campaign." The Japanese military quickly established bases there, about 1,200 miles west of the Alaskan peninsula, possibly to monitor any American attempts to strike Japan from the Aleutians, or possibly to dilute US forces before the planned Japanese strike on the more strategic Midway Island in the central Pacific. Either way, the islands represented the only US soil captured by an enemy during the war, and because of that their recapture had great symbolic value.

After setting up a naval blockade of the islands, the US military landed 11,000 troops on Attu in May 1943 to take it back. After a bloody two-day battle, 2,000 Japanese soldiers were dead, as were about 1,000 Americans. The Japanese occupiers soon abandoned Kiska, where 35,000 American soldiers landed unopposed in August 1943.

Was Biber part of that mostly uncelebrated effort? Difficult to say, though his cryptic comments to Tucker raise that intriguing possibility.

Biber excelled at a number of things during his post-war life, including his pre-medical studies to become a psychiatrist and his quest to become a member of the US Olympic weightlifting team. He once claimed to have missed that honor "by twenty pounds," and even into his eighties was prone to rolling his sleeves up over his biceps to show off his guns, or vamping a bodybuilder's pose.[8] After graduating from medical school at the University of Iowa in 1948, he discovered a talent and passion for surgery during his residency at an Army hospital in the Panama Canal zone. As a gifted pianist, he found that his dexterous hands quickly adapted to the fine motor skills needed during surgery. He liked the challenge of it and the opportunity to innovate as circumstances with the patient changed. He got good, and people noticed.

Biber eventually found himself in Korea. "He was encouraged by the government to either volunteer for two years, or be drafted for three," widow Mary Lee Biber recalls. "So he volunteered and went to the DMZ as a MASH doctor." As the unit's chief surgeon, Biber once told an interviewer, he supervised such medical advances as vessel transplants and "got a tremendous amount of experience. Tremendous." He also became an inadvertent hero, according to two family members, after accompanying a helicopter pilot behind enemy lines to rescue wounded soldiers. "He didn't know he had crossed enemy lines!" says stepdaughter Kelly Biber, whose mother, Ella Mae, was Biber's fourth wife. "He went and he picked them up. They were shooting at him and everything. And he brought them back. But he said, 'Do you think I'm dumb? I wouldn't have crossed enemy lines. I didn't know!'"

After Korea, Biber was working at the Army's Fort Carson near Colorado Springs when a colleague asked him to join a five-member clinic planned by the United Mine Workers in Trinidad. He figured he'd help get the clinic up and running, then move on. But he didn't. While Las Animas County's population peaked at nearly 39,000 people during the coal boom in the 1920s, it still had a post-boom population of about 26,000 residents by the 1950s. At that point, Biber was the only general surgeon in town.

His focus was caring for the workers doing the dangerous underground work at the Allen Mine, which opened in 1951 and was among the most productive in the state. He once told Ella Mae, to whom he was married for twenty-three years, that he knew he could practice medicine anywhere in the world. But he also told her he never wanted to leave Trinidad. "He was so dedicated there," she says. "He delivered so many babies, did everybody's surgery, and everybody trusted him tremendously. He loved everyone in Trinidad. You don't see doctors commit to their patients anymore. He took care of them from birth to death, in most cases."

Mary Lee Biber, who as a nurse worked with Biber for forty-two years before becoming his fifth wife, says she ended up marrying the man who'd been her doctor since she was fifteen years old.

Biber once described working eighteen-hour days, six days a week, during his early years in Trinidad. By many accounts, he did a bit of everything, from setting broken bones, to repairing gunshot wounds, to resolving more run-of-the-mill problems such as hernias, hemorrhoids, and appendectomies. "He told me he made $3,500 his first year in Trinidad," says Mary Lee, who once saw a copy of Biber's 1954 income tax return. "He charged three dollars for a house call and two dollars for an office visit."

He also began what ultimately would become a very complicated family life—five wives and nine children and step-children[9]—during those years as well. It would not be unfair to call him a serial marryer, but by all accounts he didn't like being alone, bonded deeply with each of the women he wed, and sincerely wanted them to share his life. He and his first wife, Shirley, had four children: Joni (who now goes by the name Prabhu Nam Kaur Khalsa), Robert, Debbie, and Patricia. After the marriage ended in divorce, Shirley decided to relocate with their kids to the Denver area, nearly 200 miles north of Trinidad. The children sometimes visited their father, and Biber apparently used his pilot's license to visit them on weekends, but for much of their lives there apparently remained a distance—geographic and emotional—between Biber and those four children.

Biber's second marriage, to Sharon, was short-lived, but produced a son, David, who now lives in a rural area near Pueblo. The surgeon's third marriage, to a nurse named Debbie, was brief as well, and produced no children. The twenty-three-year marriage to Ella Mae produced two children, John Allen and

Terri, who shared Biber's ranch home with Ella Mae's daughters from her previous marriage, Pam and Kelly. Biber spent his final years with long-time nurse Mary Lee Vigil, eventually marrying her in 2005, less than a year before his death in January 2006, at age eighty-two.

Biber's professional success carried on through it all. The more he worked, the more he got to know the people in the community, and the more useful Biber felt. He touched many lives, in many ways, every day. It's hard to find a local who's not eager to share a personal story of the time Biber set their broken bone, did minor surgery during an office visit, or delivered them squalling into the world.

Lifelong Trinidad resident Dick Hamman recalls a day in 1960 when Biber saved his father's life. The elder Hamman, a tough-it-out clerk on the Colorado and Southern Railway for nearly fifty years, experienced severe abdominal pain at work and was sent home to recuperate after four days of suffering. The family doctor requested a urine sample, which Hamman's mother collected in a sterilized jar. Young Dick, then perhaps eight or nine years old, rode the sample to the doctor's Main Street office on his bicycle. The doctor tested the sample and ordered Hamman's father to the hospital immediately.

When they arrived by car, Stanley Biber was waiting and took his father immediately into the operating room where Biber discovered that Hamman's appendix had ruptured four days before. Peritonitis had already set in. "That's a death sentence," Hamman's son says. "He took my dad in, cut him open, and literally took his guts out, put them on the table, washed them all out, repaired everything, put him back together, and sewed him up. And since then dad swore he was the best ever. Before that he didn't like Dr. Biber, but after that..."

Hamman shakes his head as he recounts the story. "Everybody will tell you he was a brilliant, brilliant surgeon. And he was. He was very good at it."

But Hamman also recalls that, as a medical doctor, Biber's bedside manner was sometimes less exemplary, and his diagnostic skills sometimes wanting—an opinion at odds with many others in town who hail Biber's skill, empathy, and compassion. "Unless he was doing surgery, you didn't want to talk to him. I could find you many people who would tell you that same, same thing. As a medical doctor, he sucked, excuse my language. But you put a scalpel in his hand, he was Michelangelo. He was the greatest."

The one aspect of Biber's personality that those who knew him bring up consistently was his relentless and, at times comic, frugality. His children and stepchildren cite as evidence "the truck," an ancient, battered Toyota pickup of indeterminate year that was handed down from child to child as they reached driving age.

Stepdaughter Kelly just rolls her eyes when she talks about the truck's complicated pedigree, and longtime financial advisor Kelly Tucker remembers Biber driving the same rattletrap vehicle one day in 1983 when he was scheduled to meet Biber at a local restaurant. "He pulls up in one of those old Toyota pickups like you see the terrorists drive," Tucker recalls. "He was just the cheapest person you'd ever meet. He had a lot of money"—Tucker won't talk specifics, but concedes Biber became a multimillionaire— "and he helped me get wealthy, too. But that office of his... it looked like a 1930s-issue state hospital. The one thing he'd spend money on was land, but he had no nice cars, no nice houses. He didn't dress well, nothing to call attention to himself. You wouldn't think he had a nickel if you saw him on the street."

Son John Biber, who lives near his mother Ella Mae, Biber's fourth wife, in Dripping Springs, Texas, laughs while recounting stories of his father's fabled frugality, saying, "he never spent money on anything but cows and acreage." Stanley Biber didn't want showers in his houses because he felt they wasted water, and John recalls how he and his siblings shared bath water well into their teens. They cut trees for firewood rather than running the boiler system in their home.

His father also had a stubborn habit of buying the cheapest work gloves he could find, usually a ten-pack he'd get for a couple of bucks at the local hardware store that would wear out in a day as they worked on fences and did other ranch work. "I can't tell you how many times I would argue with him and say, 'You know what? If you'd just buy me a nice pair of gloves, they'll last me a year or more. I'm not gonna lose them, I promise.' Looking back on it now makes me smile, but in the heat of the moment I was just, 'Why not just get the nice stuff?'"

Carol Cometto, a lifelong Trinidad resident who Biber delivered in 1961 and who for nearly two decades played on the "Doc's Patients" softball team that Biber sponsored and coached, recalls Biber always having some of his kids with him, but "never pulling out a dollar to buy them candy or soft drinks." Cometto says she often bought them treats herself.

"Cheap is not the word!" she recalls. "I'd read the paper, and he'd say, 'Carol, when you're done with the paper bring it over to the office.' It was fifteen cents!"

Fourth wife Ella Mae Biber says, "He was so tight he could squeeze a penny and turn it into copper wire."

Mary Lee, Biber's fifth and final wife, who believes she "had the best part of him" during the final years of his life, says Biber considered his life complete only if he had a wife and kids around. He didn't like being alone, and even talked to her about finding a surrogate mother so the two of them—he was then in his late seventies, she in her early sixties—could raise a child together. "He didn't like going home to an empty house," she says. "He would come home from work and yell, 'Where's my honey?' Every time he walked in the house."

Asked if Biber was romantic, though, Mary Lee Biber sighs deeply. The frugality thing again. "Let me tell you this story," she says, and recounts the time Biber told her, "Let's go get you a card for Valentine's Day!" Off they went to the card store. Once there, he told her to pick out any card she wanted. She found one she liked. "He said, 'Read it!'" When she was done, he wished her a happy Valentine's Day, put the card back on the display, and they left. Summing up, she says: "I guess he was romantic in his own way."

Biber's childhood fantasies about being a rancher suddenly seemed within reach in his early years in Trinidad. He once described how those fantasies were reignited during his visits to a local feed store, while sitting on a bale of alfalfa. "I told myself, 'Someday I'm going to get me a ranch,'" he told an interviewer in 1998.

He approached the enterprise like a businessman, buying a patch of land and starting with about twenty-five head of cattle. He bought more land, then more cattle, then more land, then more cattle—eventually assembling a collection of ranches that made the town surgeon one of the largest landowners in Las Animas County. Joe DeGarbo, president of the Trinidad branch of InBank who owns a ranch near Biber's home and mentored the doctor during his early ranching days, estimates Biber eventually purchased about eight noncontiguous ranches totaling between forty and fifty thousand acres. But watching the surgeon's learning curve was, for a while, a spectator sport in the community as Biber ate dust and broke his own bones during tumbles from horseback. He once turned over a cattle truck, injuring himself badly.

But along the way, Biber learned about the proper moisture levels in hay and pasture management. He plowed fields before reporting to Mt. San Rafael for surgeries, and frequented cattle auctions to build a herd DeGarbo estimates eventually reached between 1,500 and 1,800 head, including such diverse breeds as Black Angus, Hereford, and Limousin.

Eugene Lujan, another rancher with whom Biber later served as one of three commissioners overseeing Las Animas County, remembers accompanying Biber to a cattle auction and being startled by the criteria Biber applied when choosing bulls for his herd. Asked to explain why he'd picked one bull over another, Biber told Lujan that his chosen bull's testicles rode higher than the bull he didn't choose, and explained that he didn't want the creature's baby makers dragging in the snow. "Everybody has their own standards, I guess," Lujan says with a shrug, and given Biber's medical credentials he had no reason to argue.

The moment that would change Biber's life, the reputation of his adopted hometown, and the lives of thousands of transgender patients "came to him by accident," says stepdaughter Kelly. "It just kind of walked into his office one day."

His visitor was a friend, a social worker with whom Biber had consulted in the past on harelip and cleft palate cases from around Las Animas County. As Biber recounted in a 1998 interview, the red-haired woman lingered a moment after the business of the day was finished. Eventually, she summoned the nerve to ask a question: "Can you do my surgery?"

Biber, the battle-tested field surgeon, agreed without discussion, boasting, "Of course I can do your surgery. What do you want done?"

His visitor explained that she was a transsexual woman, Biber pondered her words for a bit, his mouth open. Finally, he spoke:

"What's that?"

In 1969, it was a reasonable response. Sure, he knew about the sensational case in which former GI George Jorgensen was surgically transformed. Who didn't? But at the time, the term transsexual was hardly part of the cultural vocabulary. Biber no doubt knew about homosexuals, and may have heard the term transvestite. But transsexual?

After his visitor explained that she was among the first patients to be treated with female hormones by pioneering gender researcher Dr. Harry Benjamin, the cocksure Biber began educating himself the same afternoon—apparently after he'd tentatively agreed to do the operation. He learned that Benjamin was a German-born protege of Magnus Hirschfeld,[10] who Susan Stryker, author of the 2008 book *Transgender History*, says first advanced the theory of "sexual intermediaries"—the notion that each person represents a unique combination of sex characteristics, secondary sex-linked traits, erotic preferences, psychological inclinations, and culturally acquired habits and practices. Benjamin moved to the US in 1913, and by the

1950s had established himself as the leading American authority on transsexuality. It would be another decade before Benjamin's "standards of care" would become the generally accepted protocol for treating transgender patients, but Biber's visitor apparently already was adhering to basic tenets of those standards. She was taking hormones, had passed Benjamin's psychological criteria for the surgery, and already had lived for a full year as a woman.

At the time, Johns Hopkins Hospital in Baltimore was the American center of what then was called "sex-change surgery." Biber called Dr. John Hoopes, a plastic surgeon at Johns Hopkins who at the time had done about thirteen such operations, seven of which were what Biber described as "simple penectomies" similar to the operation done on Jorgensen. Hoopes eventually sent Biber a set of rudimentary hand-drawn diagrams—imagine sketches done by a precocious sixth-grader who had some experience doing prostate and gynecological surgery—showing the basic technique for deconstructing a man's genitalia and reconstructing it into a sort of artisanal vagina. Biber looked over the drawings and called the social worker back. "Well, I've never done one, but if you want to do it, I think we can do it."

She agreed, and Biber for the first time performed a procedure known as the penile-scrotal flap, a technique he later described as "horrible looking." But he also said it seemed to work reasonably well.

In the early 1970s, transgender people seeking surgical relief didn't have many options. Things were changing, for sure. Thanks to the social and sexual upheavals of the 1960s, women wearing pants in public no longer caused a fuss, and men whose hair spilled over their collar were more the norm than the exception. Gender-bending entertainers such as the New York Dolls and David Bowie were finding their way into the American mainstream. Historian Susan Stryker describes the dawning of a momentarily cool "transgender aesthetic" back then that signaled a changing relationship between appearance and biological sex, even if the more entrenched forms of gender discrimination and sexism remained firmly in place. For transgender men and women such as Claudine Griggs and Walt Heyer, Stanley Biber's nascent practice in Trinidad was a revelation. Here was a skilled surgeon at a real hospital who offered them help, dignity, and hope—all with a dose of unflappable confidence, and without judgment. At the time, that combination was enough to coax reluctant and sometimes desperate people like them to Trinidad from thousands of miles away.

How powerful was the appeal? Powerful enough, Griggs says, to overcome her first impressions of Biber's spartan fourth-floor office above Trinidad's First National Bank. She sensed an empathy in Biber, who in 1998 told writer Harrison Fletcher of Denver's *Westword* magazine: "No amount of psychological help can change a true transsexual. The longer you work with these people, the more you develop empathy. You realize how hard it really is for them."

Griggs says her initial take on the surgeon was colored by the pre-surgery enthusiasm of her UCLA endocrinologist, Dr. Gerald Leve. "He had praised Biber so much for his skill and compassion and generosity in working with trans patients in Trinidad that I felt a great relief. I'd been working with Dr. Leve for almost twenty years at that time, and I valued his opinion enough that I was confident in Biber's skill and that I'd be treated well, although it was hard to believe I'd be treated well because of experiences I'd had."

The terror she felt leading up to her first meeting with Biber was based mostly on her fear that he would reject her as a surgical candidate and send her back to Southern California just as she had arrived. "I was a surgical *candidate,* but I still wondered if I would go home without that surgery, which to me was a matter of life and death. I was terrified of being rejected. But I remember feeling very confident in him as a surgeon; he seemed very mild-mannered, down-to-earth, and absolutely sure of himself. So that was a great relief."

She was equally reassured by her first glimpse of Mt. San Rafael Hospital when she arrived. "When I was driving there, I couldn't imagine how a town as small as Trinidad could actually have a real medical facility and do these kinds of surgeries.

So the first thing I did was drive by the hospital. It actually looked like a hospital, and I was very relieved."

To Griggs, Heyer, and the thousands like them who journeyed to Trinidad to see Stanley Biber, the man was so much more than a skilled surgeon. He was a beacon, a believer, a man who seemed to know intuitively in 1969 what decades of scientific research now affirm: The pain of gender dysphoria is real and often devastating—but relief is possible.

5

The Elevator

Five days before her thirty-eighth birthday, Claudine Griggs and Carolyn, her companion and lover at the time, entered the side entrance to Trinidad's First National Bank building. Griggs was nervous, terrified actually, as she boarded the narrow, rattletrap elevator to Biber's private office for her 9:30 a.m. evaluation appointment. She didn't notice that the renaissance revival building's imposing sandstone facade along East Main and South Commercial streets is little more than that—a facade. While those edifices convey the sober seriousness of a key financial anchor for the community, the other two sides of the structure, the back and the east-facing wall, are ordinary painted brick. From one angle, the building looks like a First National Bank building should, with its gracefully arched front entrance, modern windows, and blocky stone. From another, the flecking paint, window air conditioners, and zig-zagging grey metal fire escape say nothing so much as "New York tenement." The building where Biber chose to locate his private office—the epicenter of Trinidad's downtown for nearly a century and a half, starting with serving pioneers along the Santa Fe Trail in 1875—itself has some identity issues.

By then, Griggs had the hardened psychological armor of a lifelong transsexual. She'd mistrusted doctors since her earliest attempts to find a capable and compassionate surgeon, and stepping into the elevator was the biggest and scariest step she would ever take. Amplifying the anxiety of the moment was her general mistrust of men, for reasons stemming from a brutal experience when she was twenty-one years old. She recounts the incident without tears—not detached exactly, but in a tone from which the anger and bitterness seems to have been leached. What's left of the story more than four decades later is like a river rock, smoothed by time and without hard edges.

It happened just months after she first began living as a woman. She'd finished high school as Claude and served a year and a half as a journalist and broadcaster in the US Air Force until her career there began to wobble. She was struggling with her gender identity, though she never mentioned that to her Air Force psychiatrists. She was suicidal, though, and was sent home for eighteen months to recover. She returned from that hiatus prepared to complete her tour of duty, but confided in a psychologist handling her evaluation that she was transgender and that she eventually planned to undergo gender confirmation surgery. The psychologist was sympathetic and considered her mentally stable, she recalls, but predicted correctly that Air Force policy at the time would prevail. She was honorably discharged six weeks later. Still just twenty, she was uncertain about her future, but absolutely certain of her gender identity.

As Claude, and taking advantage of her GI Bill education benefits, she'd begun studying at Chaffey College in Alta Loma, California. While not trying to pass as female at that point, she easily could have. Griggs had no visible body hair and very little facial hair, and she'd begun to develop small breasts long before she began hormone therapy. Those ambiguous physical characteristics, combined with her slight five-foot-five, one-hundred-twenty-pound frame, promised a relatively seamless transition from male to female. She took off one quarter from college, began hormone therapy in May 1974, and began living as a woman on July 1 that year. She reentered Chaffey that summer as Claudine.

As a transgender coed with a secret, the slight, attractive Griggs and had no trouble drawing the attention of male classmates. Her studio portrait as a high school senior in 1971 shows a handsome young man with short hair and kind eyes, with a toothy grin she now says was forced, masking the depression and inner torment she experienced as a transgender teenager. It's a striking contrast to the 1977 portrait of her as a student at California State Polytechnic University in Pomona, from which she graduated with a Bachelor of Arts in English in 1978. That later picture shows a confident young woman in the unisex style of the era, with long, middle-parted blond hair and a maroon turtleneck sweater. The smile seems infinitely more genuine.

It was that way from the start of her transition. "Within a week or two, people were asking me out, and I was very surprised," she recalls. "I didn't expect anybody (to do that) because I thought I was too ugly. I thought I was the most hideous woman around, and I couldn't understand that other people didn't see me that way."

Within a couple of months of her reentry to Chaffey, one of those courtships led to her first sexual encounter with a man who she says seemed comfortable with her in-between gender status. But not long after that, things took a dark turn. She'd called his house and was told by her boyfriend's roommate that her boyfriend was out. The roommate invited her over, assuring her that her lover would be back shortly. But the boyfriend was not there when she arrived. The roommate invited her in. A second man was hiding behind the door as she entered, she says, and "things went downhill from there."

She remembers one of the men gesturing to a coffee table, where she saw a large knife she compares to the one featured in the shower scene of Alfred Hitchcock's *Psycho*. She knew at that moment she was in trouble. The mood shifted. Just twenty-one, her goal suddenly became survival, nothing more, and she was immediately convinced that cooperation gave her the best odds of getting out of the apartment alive.

The assault lasted several hours, and she remembers having the same classic out-of-body experience described by many rape victims. At one point, one of her assailants struck her. She doesn't remember feeling it, but she remembers hearing it and thinking, "Oh, he just hit me." At another point, one of the men burned her with a lit cigarette "when I wasn't enthusiastic enough." She remembers thinking, I sure hope a child is not the one who finds my body in the dumpster somewhere. She still recalls one of her assailants' parting words when the ordeal was over: "Since you want to be a woman, you should thank me for this."

She apparently drove herself home, though she has no memory of that. She does remember crawling up the stairs to her apartment, humiliated and wracked by pain. Her instincts told her to call the police, but her experience with discrimination as a transgender woman convinced her otherwise. She thought, *No, the police will rape me too when they find out I'm trans.*

Instead of making the call, she drew a bath, almost intolerably hot, and climbed in. She scrubbed her skin until it hurt, trying to rid herself of the smell of her attackers. Then she went to bed and allowed herself to cry. In the sometimes absurd, hall-of-mirrors reality of growing up transgender, she recalls being angry with her mother for never warning her that men could be such predators. But of course, her mother had raised what she thought was a son, and so the precautionary mother-daughter conversation about dating had never happened. So Griggs tamped down her pain and anger, never reported the crime to the police, and kept the secret even from her therapist for more than two decades—until she alluded to it in the published 1996 journal of her transition.

To this day, she doesn't know whether the man she was dating was aware of the rape plan. But he never called her after that, so she suspects he knew—an unfathomable betrayal by her very first lover, a scar that has never faded.

Her experiences were hardly unique, of course. Among transgender men and women back then, and even now, hostility, violence, and desperation are daily realities. She'd read articles about people like her being beaten to death in jail while guards looked on, about paramedics who allowed someone like her to bleed to death at a car accident scene, joking as it happened. Someone once anonymously mailed Griggs a copy of an article about a transgender woman in Great Britain who died after being bound with chains and weights and then dropped into the sea. She's still not sure if the sender's scribbled message—"Be careful, Claudine"—was a warning or a threat.

On top of those personal horrors was her general disdain for herself as a transsexual,[11] which she later described this way: "Transsexualism is a bad accident on the other side of the freeway. No matter how horrible it may be for the people involved, bystanders must inevitably slow down to take a gander. It's not malicious; it's just a kind of horrific show that's too good to pass over. They think, 'What a mess! I'm glad I'm not involved,' and step forcefully on the accelerator to speed past once they've had a good look. Real tragedies remain, however. Those affected must pick up broken lives and carry on, if they are able, occasionally noting the glances of those who drive by."

She also compared her options as a transsexual woman to choices that always seemed to involve the lesser of evils. She hated trying to live as a man, but found the idea of surgery no less repellent. Surgery, or suicide? "The great sleep might have been preferable," she remembers thinking. "How does one judge?"

So Griggs was carrying a lot of emotional baggage as she stepped anxiously into that claustrophobic elevator. And yet she did so with unwavering resolve. "I was so used to being treated badly when people knew I was transsexual. I was used to being mistreated in life-threatening ways, sometimes. Whenever I was the center of attention, it usually meant violence was coming, or insults, or something bad was going to happen. So coming from that background, where being trans could get you killed, to be in a place where they knew and were actually trying to help, it was remarkable to me."

For the appointment, Griggs decided to forego her preferred jeans and sweatshirt for dress slacks and a white blouse—what she later described in her journal as "at least a modest attempt at femininity." She was second-guessing a lot of things, worried that if she didn't look feminine enough Biber might conclude that she hadn't adjusted well to living as a woman. She and Carolyn were joined in the small elevator by a woman who turned out to be Biber's secretary, who a few minutes later would conduct the first part of Griggs's screening interview.

During that conversation, the secretary had Griggs sign a consent form, do some paperwork related to her name change, and turn over the results of her AIDS test. She then asked Griggs for a cashier's check made out to Dr. Biber for the agreed-upon $4,350 and wrote out a receipt for that amount plus the $500 deposit that Griggs already had paid. Then, some post-op instructions: Griggs was to drink lots of fluids, avoid heavy lifting, and promise not to return to work for six weeks after surgery. She also told Griggs to visit a local adult bookstore before the operation to purchase what she called a large dilator—you probably know it by the less clinical term "dildo"—to be used to help dilate and expand the interior of her new vagina, which Biber would fashion from the somewhat elastic, nerve-packed skin of her severed penis. The hospital would provide two smaller dilators to keep the vagina open while it healed, the secretary explained, but the larger one would be needed to deepen it, making it functional for sexual penetration.

The interview didn't last long, and the secretary reminded Griggs that she was due back at the office at 11:00 that morning for her evaluation meeting with Dr. Biber, "one of the most important persons in my life, someone I have never met before, someone I will probably never see again after I leave Trinidad," she later wrote in her journal. "But I will carry the results of our meeting for the rest of my life. I am excited. I am terrified."

The terror subsided when she met her surgeon, who had just arrived at the office after performing a morning surgery at Mt. San Rafael. Biber seemed warm and upbeat, and proceeded quickly through a series of questions intended to gauge Griggs's fitness for the operation. They were familiar; Griggs answered many of them in the written social history she'd mailed to Biber six months before, as requested: How long have you lived as a woman? Do you consider yourself happy? How long have you been taking hormones? Any adverse effects from the hormones? Does your family support this decision? Ever been married? Children?

One of Biber's questions in particular sounded off-key to Griggs: *How many times have you attempted suicide?* Why didn't he ask *whether* she had ever attempted suicide? Not that she hadn't considered ending her life. She had. Still, his phrasing struck her as presumptuous.[12] But Biber had met a lot of transgender patients since he began doing the surgeries in 1969. Maybe it was the breadth of his experience, or perhaps the intuition upon which he seemed to rely, but he phrased the question the way he did without explanation or apology.

When he finished, Biber invited Griggs to step into an adjoining room for a physical examination. Like the rest of the office, the room was spartan: an exam table, a chair, a storage cabinet. Griggs noticed that the single window had no curtains, and Biber told her not to worry about being seen, since they were on the top floor of the tallest building in town. Before excusing himself for a few moments, he asked her to completely undress.

Griggs hesitated and took several deep breaths. Revealing her whole body, with what she describes as its "disturbing incongruity" of developed breasts and male genitalia, was always a trauma. "I still hate that part of my body which is explicitly male," she would later write in her journal. "Even its diminished size and functional capacity, from years of estrogen therapy, have not tempered my enmity toward this organ." But eventually she began to disrobe. Biber returned just as she finished removing her panties and bra.

"He was very casual about it, and that casualness was one of the most reassuring things," she remembers. "That was later reinforced as he treated me. His whole team was reassuring that way. Everybody talked about Biber as, 'Don't worry. Everything is gonna be fine.' But having met him there in that office, I felt like, 'OK, I'm going through with this.' And that was good to know. He was a mixture of Genghis Khan and Huck Finn—he had the decency and honesty of Huck Finn, but he also had that imperious confidence, which is probably something I needed more than anything else at that time."

Biber slipped a pressurized sleeve onto Griggs's arm and conducted a blood pressure test—it was a little high— and concluded that it was probably because she was nervous. He checked her eyes, ears, throat, and heart. He examined her breasts, and together they agreed there was no reason to consider breast implants. She remembers his examination of her penis as a little rough, a practical and unceremonious handling by a tradesman.

She knew he was considering the organ as a seamstress might consider a piece of fabric. Is there enough material to make what needs to be made? For some male-to-female surgical candidates, Biber needed to supplement the penis skin with a swatch of skin taken from the buttocks in order to create a fully functional vagina. But doing so risked complications, and Biber preferred to avoid the skin graft whenever possible. In Griggs's case, it was a toss-up. The surgeon estimated there was enough skin to create a vagina that would be three to three-and-a-half inches deep, and says if Griggs is consistent with her painful daily dilations, her vagina depth could expand to five or six inches during the six to eight months after surgery. The decision, he said, was hers.

Griggs chose the less risky option, foregoing the skin graft. ("I have been patient all of my life. Like Siddhartha, I learned to wait," she says.)

With that, the physical exam was over. Biber left the room as Griggs got dressed, and she found him at his desk in the main office scribbling notes. He motioned for her to sit, and she did. He asked a few more questions, proclaimed "Tomorrow is your day! Everything is going to be fine!" and then launched into a litany of possible complications from the surgery. There was the potential for death, of course, and the risk of infection common with any surgical procedure. Also, he told her, you may lose parts of your newly built labia (fashioned from scrotum skin) and clitoris (made from sensitive, nerve-rich skin at the head of the penis). A hole might develop between the vagina and the rectum, the most serious potential problem other than the death thing. Oh, and depending on the breaks, you may never achieve orgasm. But Biber added that, after more than 2,000 surgeries, he'd pretty much worked out the kinks. "Most of the problems occurred in our early surgeries, while we were still learning how to do it," he said, predicting Griggs would do just fine and walk out of Mt. San Rafael after nine days feeling like, well, a new woman.

Thus informed, Griggs consented.

After taking a few 35mm photographs of the fully clothed Griggs for his records, Biber directed her to the nearby hospital for admission.

The afternoon passed in a blur of paperwork, blood testing, additional money exchanges (for the hospital and anesthesiologist fees), room assignment, and a quick tour of the facilities. At one point, near the end of a hallway, Griggs passed a double door with a sign that read: "Surgery—No Visitors." Projecting herself beyond those doors, her emotions begin to swirl. When she finally reached her assigned room, Room 444, she collapsed into a small upholstered chair at the end of the bed. She recalled the moment in her journal:

"For almost 15 years, after I gave up trying to find a surgeon, I disclosed to almost no one that I am transsexual; I've existed at work, at home, at school, in the shopping mall, grocery store, bowling alley, golf course, library, on the freeways, on the sidewalks, every place but the bedroom and the doctor's office, Mondays through Sundays, year after year, with no one apparently knowing that I'm not just a girl down the street. Now, in the last couple of days, I've had to confront the fact that I am transsexual with a dozen people I've never previously met, and soon I'll have to face that situation again."

The surgery promised to make things different, she knew, the only "livable path" before her. But she also understood it was not guaranteed to make things better. "Tomorrow, I remain transsexual, and my body will ache as well. A predictably rotten alliance."

But in the quiet of her hospital room, with no one asking questions, no one examining or probing, she felt a momentary relief. Griggs knew her long effort to maintain her privacy was a choice, her choice, and that this relatively public stage of her transition was probably more difficult because of that. She found herself wishing she'd been able to better deal with the self-loathing about her life as a transsexual woman. That's not something she could change, but during her first twenty-four hours in Trinidad, she later wrote, she'd been surrounded by people who constantly reminded her that "I am what I hate."

It was exhausting.

Her respite didn't last long. More staffers, more questions. Allergic to any medications? What hormones are you taking? Diabetic? Previous surgeries? A rattling cart was rolled into the room. It contained a small television and a videotape player. She was instructed to watch three videos, two of which were standard for all hospital patients, and a third created strictly for patients like her. It included an interview with Dr. Biber, and a recap of his role in making Trinidad a world center for gender confirmation surgery. An attendant assured her that "It's nothing gross," and indeed Griggs found it comforting.

As the day before her surgery drew to a close, the ever-literary Claudine Griggs found herself thinking about a Tom Joad quote from *The Grapes of Wrath*: "It don't take no nerve to do somepin when there ain't nothin' else you can do." She had arrived at a point where she felt like she had no options. "And I really looked for the third option," she recalls. "I wanted something else. And I wanted it even before I changed my name back in 1974. I said, 'OK, I know I have a feminine gender identity. I know that I'm male. What alternative is there besides suffering with it, or going through sex reassignment?' I'd read everything I could find, every psychological monograph, every microfilm at the college, looking for articles. I read about suicide rates among transsexuals. And I wanted the third option, something that didn't involve either living as a man, or going through a sex change. If you find it, tell people about it. I don't know what it is."

She had concluded surgery was the best road possible, even though it was still horrible, even though she wasn't convinced she'd survive it. The idea of living as a woman with male genitalia disgusted her. And she also knew surgery would not solve all her problems. She already could pass as a woman among anyone who saw her clothed. But her situation was so much more complicated than that. She'd still have to figure out how to deal with being a transsexual woman for life. There'd still be family issues, relationship issues, medical issues. Those are things no surgery could remove. "If I worked and got twelve PhDs, I'm still gonna be trans," she recalls thinking. "It really bothered me that there was no way to get over that."

She thought, too, of the psychologist she saw years earlier, someone with whom she once discussed her options during a deep depression. "When I was desperately depressed and told a psychologist that I really didn't want to go through a sex change—it's just horrible, the idea of it—he said, 'Well, you can try it, and if you don't like it, you can always still kill yourself and you'll be at the same place you would have been.' And that was the perfect logic for me."

6

The second time Walt Heyer arrived in Trinidad, in April 1983, he did so with more resolve than during his first disastrous visit two years earlier. But his behavior leading up to that point had become increasingly erratic despite having embraced Christianity with sincere fervor. Deep inside him, Jesus was waging a fierce battle with the woman he felt inhabited his body, whom he had begun calling Andrea West.

Andrea was winning, especially when he was home alone following the divorce precipitated by his decision to sneak away to have a Lake Tahoe cosmetic surgeon give him breast implants. Preparing for gender confirmation surgery, he'd begun preparing his body, at least superficially, for life as a woman. He'd had buttocks implants, a nose job, and painful electrolysis to remove his facial hair. Even so, his resolve sometimes wavered. At one point during his pre-surgical internal struggle, he'd had his breast implants removed. Then he had them replaced. He's now lost track of how many times that happened.

His drinking also got more intense, to the point where he says his favorite bar mounted a plaque bearing his name above his favorite barstool. Honda had moved him back to Southern California in 1981. At home, alone, he'd drink until he blacked out. He hated himself for betraying his wife and two children by secretly pursuing surgery, then shattering their lives by confessing that desire. He was, in short, a mess.

The second time he arrived in Trinidad, he was convinced the time had come to follow through with the surgery that Andrea was demanding, and which his therapist had convinced him would solve his gender dysphoria problem. He didn't hesitate to climb aboard the rickety elevator to Stanley Biber's office. He didn't hesitate during the check-in process, during which he signed various medical forms as Andrea West. He had come for relief and wasn't thinking much about the long-term con-sequences or implications of that decision. He compares his compulsion at the time to a bulldozer "pushing me relentless-ly and single-mindedly toward surgery, while destroying every obstacle in its way." He lied, he manipulated, he rationalized. Eventually, the only people to whom he chose to listen were those urging him into the surgical suite. But he could see no further into his future than the surgery.

Looking back, he says his "baffling and incomprehensible" post-op plan probably made perfect sense to the alcoholic he was at the time. He intended to live simultaneously as two peo-ple—Walt, who would continue to work as a male, and Andrea West, the female persona he used during his off-work time. "This way I thought both the female and the male could each reign supreme, and my conflict would be resolved," he wrote years later. "This seemed very logical and workable."

Again, this is pretty much the exact opposite of the typical dysphoric experience.

He told his boss at Honda he needed two to three weeks off for gallbladder surgery—a cover story that was, at least partly, true. He did need gallbladder surgery. But what Heyer actual-ly had in mind was doubly brutal: He'd travel to Trinidad for gender confirmation surgery on Tuesday, then check himself out of Mt. San Rafael four days later (Biber's recommended in-hospital recovery period was six days) for a flight back to California. The following Monday, just six days after entering Biber's surgical suite, he planned to drive a hundred miles to a California hospital to prep for gallbladder surgery. He would give himself a week after both operations to recover at a sup-portive friend's beach house, then go back to work.

But the ill-considered simplicity of his post-op plan first went off the rails as he filled out the pre-op paperwork at Mt. San Rafael. A staffer asked him for the name he intended to use in his post-op life as a woman. To that point, he'd been Walt Heyer, Christal West, and Andrea West.

"Laura Jensen," he replied. He says now that the name had "no significance whatsoever. It just popped into my head."

It's too simple to attribute Heyer's impulsiveness at that stage of his life to alcohol and drugs. Those were just his way of coping with what he, like Claudine Griggs, recognized as relentless and searing pain, a constant quest for relief. He claims he didn't know a single person offering an alternative to what he was about to do.

"You get to a point where the pain that you've been suffering for over thirty-five years becomes much more important to resolve than the consequences that you might face," Heyer recalls. "I'm not sure the consequences were a total surprise. In the back of my mind I knew all these [complications] could come about, but you just don't want them to. The consequences weren't enough to stop me from moving forward."

7

Genitalia, Gender, and Sexuality

Many of us grew up in a world where gender identity was a fairly simple binary equation—someone is either male or female, or some slight variation from that presumed norm, based on outward physical characteristics. Turns out, reality is way more complicated than that. Science laid waste to that limited view of gender a long time ago, but long-ingrained cultural presumptions and prejudices are slow to change.

But things *are* changing. Look no further than Facebook, which has added a "Custom" button to its pull-down menu for users' gender identification, allowing them to describe themselves as agender, bigender, cisgender, pangender, genderqueer, androgyne, intersex, or any other of the countless now-acknowledged variations. Not sure what to make of the social media platform's related question "What pronoun do you use?" or choices that include male ("Wish him a happy birthday!), female ("Wish her a happy birthday!"), and neutral ("Wish them a happy birthday!")? Join the crowd. So, let's start with some basics.

Life begins, for all of us, as a cluster of cells without any sexual anatomy whatsoever. In utero, our unformed genitalia all look pretty much the same—an opening near the anus with a small genital bud that works as a fleshy bit of raw material, like modeling clay. Add proper amounts of the right hormones (testosterone and others) and that bud eventually shapes itself into a functioning penis and scrotum. Add different hormones (estrogen and others) and the opening develops into a vagina and labia, with the bud becoming the clitoris. This begins to happen about eleven weeks after conception. Says one notable California ob-gyn specializing in transgender issues: "We all come from the same soup.

"There's an expression in biology that says, 'Ontogeny recapitulates phylogeny,' which essentially means from the time we come together as embryos we go through the entire history of evolution," she says. "When it comes to genitals, everyone starts with basically a female substructure. People think men are from Mars and women are from Venus, and that's just simply not the case."

Our twenty-three pairs of chromosomes are arranged along a chain, and only one of those pairs—the last link in the chain— determines whether we'll become genetic males (XY) or genetic females (XX). You can safely assume that once the hormonal spice is sprinkled, male genitals and female genitals develop along some standard gender-specific path to become either a penis and testicles, or a vagina, because most do. But that's not always the case.

By the time we're born, there's a good possibility—a 1 in 100 chance, according to Brown University researcher Anne Fausto-Sterling—that our sexual anatomy will differ in some way from what we think of as standard-issue male and female genitalia. Other research suggests that as many as 1.7 percent of people are born with "intersex" characteristics that are some subtle form of sex anatomy variation—roughly the same ratio as the number of redheads in the human population. A genetic male may, for example, have a micropenis where the original bud never fully developed; or very small or undescended testicles; or a common condition known as hypospadias, where the opening of the penis is on the underside of the shaft rather than at the tip, much like the urinary opening in females. This happens in about half of one percent of the human population.

Conversely, a genetic female may be born with an enlarged clitoris resembling a micropenis, without ovaries, or as is the case with intersex South African sprinter Caster Semenya, naturally occurring testosterone levels that are above the recognized "normal" level for female athletes. That biological reality, along with the fact that she's a female with XY chromosomes, has kept Semenya's career as a two-time Olympic 800-meter champion under intense scrutiny. In spring 2019, the Court of Arbitration for Sport upheld a ruling by the International Association of Athletics Federation that put Semenya in the impossible position of either taking medications to decrease her testosterone levels in order to compete against women, competing against men, or not competing at all on the world stage for female athletes. The court embraced the laughable notion that there are only two genders, and that the dividing line between the two is the precise measurement of a hormone in the blood. But as biologists continue to expand our understanding about the fluidity of gender, the walls of those rigid, long-held gender boxes begin to crumble. The more we learn, the harder it becomes to define a "normal" male or female athlete.

The Intersex Society of North America explains it this way:

> Intersex is a socially constructed category that reflects real biological variation. To better explain this, we can liken the sex spectrum to the color spectrum. There's no question that in nature there are different wavelengths that translate into colors most of us see as red, blue, orange, yellow. But the decision to distinguish, say, between orange and red-orange is made only when we need it—like when we're asking for a particular paint color. Sometimes social necessity leads us to make color distinctions that otherwise would seem incorrect or irrational, as, for instance, when we call certain people "black" or "white" when they're not especially black or white as we would otherwise use the terms.
>
> In the same way, nature presents us with sex anatomy spectrums. Breasts, penises, clitorises, scrotums, labia, gonads—all of these vary in size and shape and morphology. So-called "sex" chromosomes can vary quite a bit, too. But in human cultures, sex categories get simplified into male, female, and sometimes intersex, in order to simplify social interactions, express what we know and feel, and maintain order.

Now, no one would blame you for thinking that a discussion about genitalia is also a discussion about gender and sexuality. But it's not. Your genitals, your gender, and your sexual orientation are all different things. Think of genitalia as one *indicator* of gender, much the same way that a speedometer is an indicator of a car. True, a speedometer can be an important and recognizable part of a car, but it's hardly the whole picture. A car is a vastly more complex collection of critical parts that together constitute what we all recognize as a car, with many of those parts far more important than the speedometer. Writer Amy Ellis Nutt described it this way in her 2015 book, *Becoming Nicole,* about a transgender identical twin:

> Sexual anatomy and gender identity are the products of two different processes, occurring at distinctly different times and along different neural pathways before we are even born. Both are functions of genes as well as hormones, and while sexual anatomy and gender identity usually match, there are dozens of biological events that can affect the outcome of the latter and cause an incongruence between the two.

In other words, sex and genitals are the product of biology, of genes and flesh and hormones. But gender identity is an interplay of flesh, hormones, socialization, and something vastly more important—the brain. Sexual orientation? Nutt quotes one scientist, "Lesson number one: Sexual orientation is who you go to bed *with*. Gender identity is who you go to bed *as*."

In *Becoming Nicole*, Nutt explains how one twin's brain developed as a male and the other as a female, even though their bodies and genitalia were pretty much the same. Susan Stryker, author of *Transgender History*, points out that some cultures, including many Native American ones, identify three or more social genders, and that often social gender is attributed to the work one does rather than the body one does it with. "The important things to bear in mind are that gender is historical (it changes over time), that it varies from place to place and culture to culture, and that it is contingent—that is, it depends on many different and seemingly unrelated things coming together in a unique and particular way."

And yet, when obstetricians, midwives, or other birth assistants welcome us into the world, they generally make an on-the-spot gender identification after a quick glance between our legs. Got a penis? Male. Got a vagina? Female. Got something in between? OK, time for a chat with the anxious parents about the implications of the term "intersex." But as science has now shown, that approach is a blunt instrument, like extrapolating from a single speedometer that the vehicle in question is a rusted green 1952 International Harvester L110 half-ton pickup truck. Genitals certainly suggest a gender identity, but they're hardly the sole determining factor. And sometimes those most obvious fleshy bits reflect the exact opposite of how an individual identifies themselves. As Stryker writes, "Rather than being an objective quality of the body (defined by sex), gender is constituted by all of the innumerable acts of performing it: how we dress, move, speak, touch, look. Gender is like a language we use to communicate ourselves to others and to understand ourselves."

It helps to think of gender not in terms of either/or, but rather in terms of the spectrum to which the Intersex Society of North America alludes. Says one California ob-gyn: "What is unknown to most of the world out there is that there is a great span of conditions that are intersex, or in between." And even beyond the ones that are already known, we see enormous diversity. And with the brain being infinitely more complex, it's not surprising that one's sense of gender is also represented by diversity."

That diversity expresses itself in many ways, but let's focus on two broad categories: gender non-conformity and gender dysphoria. Gender non-conformity[13] refers to the extent to which a person's gender identity, role, or expression differs from the cultural norms prescribed for people of a particular sex. That can be a girl who says she feels more like a boy, a teenage boy who describes himself as gender fluid, or an adult who feels physical attraction without regard to biological sex, gender, or gender identity. Those people have begun describing their unique gender experiences in specific terms, such as gender non-conforming and non-binary or genderqueer.[14] The most fortunate of those people eventually get comfortable in their skin regardless of cultural norms and become whomever they are.

Gender dysphoria, on the other hand, refers to discomfort or distress that's caused by a discrepancy between a person's gender identity and that person's sex assigned at birth. Those people struggle to reconcile their physical body with the person they feel themselves to be, and sometimes the distress it causes "meets criteria for a formal diagnosis that might be classified as a mental disorder," according to the seventh edition of the Standards of Care published by the World Professional Association for Transgender Health. The WPATH standards also note that only some gender non-conforming people experience gender dysphoria at some point in their lives.

The primary goal of medicine is to relieve suffering, and as scientists learned more about gender dysphoria since the middle of the twentieth century they began to realize that there was no one-size-fits-all approach to treating it. Some gender dysphoric people need only hormone therapy to find relief. Others need a combination of hormones and surgical intervention. Some don't need either. Some need psychotherapy. In recent years, treatment has become increasingly individualized.

Generally, a gender dysphoric person's arrival at a surgeon's office comes after years of dissonance between his or her body and mind. It's not so much the starting point for a new life as the final stage of resolving the conflict with which they have lived thus far, often with enormous difficulty and personal pain. And the fact is, the physical process of changing a man's body into a woman's, or vice versa, is a fairly uncomplicated exercise in flesh sculpting—though not for the faint of heart. "By the time they get to me, they've already completed their gender identity change," Stanley Biber told *Empire Magazine* writer Karen Evans in 1983. "I simply add the accoutrements of anatomy."

A lot of good science suggests that surgery and hormone treatments do help nearly all trans men and women, and today they're part of an accepted protocol for treating patients with gender dysphoria. Even Johns Hopkins Hospital, which in 1965 became the first academic institution to offer gender-affirming surgical procedures but stopped offering those services in 1979, recently announced that it "will soon begin providing gender-affirming surgery as another important element of our overall care program, reflecting careful consideration over the past year of best practices and the appropriate provision of care for transgender individuals."

Vocal opponents often dismiss the accumulating data and such public reconsiderations, insisting that the surgery is merely a cosmetic fix for deeper psychological issues. Countless books have been written advocating one point of view over the other. Both sides occasionally cite data that supports their arguments, and often ignore data that doesn't. And yet, understanding the surgeries is a critical part of understanding the difficult choice that so many transgender patients are willing to make.

So what actually happens in an operating suite such as Dr. Stanley Biber's, or any other surgeon specializing in gender confirmation surgery?

While modern surgeons have refined and created their own techniques, all owe a debt to Georges Burou, a French gynecologist who pioneered the basic male-to-female surgery in 1956 at his Clinique du Parc in Casablanca, Morocco. The rudimentary drawings Biber received from surgeon John Hoopes at Johns Hopkins while he was researching the technique in 1969 apparently were based on—if not actual copies of—drawings used by Burou.[15]

For a male-to-female operation, the surgeon removes the testicles and the spongy tissue inside the penis. The urethra is truncated and rearranged into a female anatomical position. To craft a functional vagina, the surgeon creates a cavity in the perineum—the fleshy bridge between the anus and the genitalia—and lines it with the sensitive and somewhat elastic outer skin from the penis that has been stretched to its limits.

Patients with particularly small penises can augment the flesh of the vaginal lining and increase its depth by opting for a skin graft from elsewhere on their body. Nerve endings remain undamaged during the procedure, allowing more than eighty percent of male-to-female patients to achieve orgasm. The empty, wrinkled scrotum is then fashioned into a labia. Some male-to-female patients opt for other custom feminizing work, such as electrolysis to remove facial hair, shaving down the throat cartilage called the Adam's apple that's common in men, and breast implants to finish the work often begun by hormone treatments. The male-to-female surgery itself is followed by months of often painful daily dilation procedures.

For anatomical females undergoing female-to-male surgeries—a far less common procedure due to the complexity and effectiveness of the genital surgery—the surgeon generally reduces the breasts and removes the ovaries and uterus. Using a transplanted flap of skin from the abdomen, the surgeon uses intricate microsurgical techniques to shape it into a tube, extends the urethra through the middle of that tube, and transplants the clitoris and other nerve endings into the end of the phallus, hoping to give the patient a chance at achieving orgasm. Many surgeons also place silicone implants inside the labia skin to simulate a scrotum.

As you may already have guessed, female-to-male surgery is a far more complicated procedure, often requiring several stages to complete. Even so, some suggest the cultural transition may be easier for those born female who transition to life as a male. In a culture that celebrates feminine beauty, "women's appearances get more attention, women's actions are commented on and critiqued more than men, so in that world it just makes sense that people will focus more on trans women than trans men," transgender activist and author of *Whipping Girl* Julia Serano told *Time* magazine in 2016.

Regardless, the patient's brain remains unchanged. The implications of that are far-ranging. A patient who struggles with depression before surgery, for example, is likely to struggle with depression after surgery. A patient who is attracted to males before surgery is probably going to remain attracted to males, and vice versa, though trying to categorize the sexuality of transgender men and women can be a challenge. Gender confirmation surgery may be the most significant, irreversible, and consequential aspect of the transgender experience, but those who approach it as a solution to all of their problems are likely to be disappointed. And yet, the surgery is considered by most scientists to be therapeutic and a step toward a reconciled and often happier existence. But like everything else in the transgender universe, it's complicated.

In her memoir *Journal of a Sex Change*, Claudine Griggs wrote about her "enmity" toward her male genitalia, describing it as an "amicable enemy." She described her decision to seek surgery as "the final attempt to cure an incurable affliction." In November 2018, essayist and critic Andrea Long Chu described the feeling of dysphoria in a *New York Times* opinion piece less than a week before her scheduled surgery: "Dysphoria feels like being unable to get warm, no matter how many layers you put on. It feels like hunger without appetite. It feels like getting on an airplane to fly home, only to realize mid-flight that this is it: You're going to spend the rest of your life on an airplane. It feels like grieving. It feels like having nothing to grieve."

Chu also conceded that those who believe transitioning will make them feel better often are wrong, describing how much worse she felt since starting hormone treatment, and how her suicidal thoughts increased rather than decreased. And yet, she had no doubt that she was doing the right thing by going through with the operation. "I tell you this not because I'm cruising for sympathy, but to prepare you for what I'm telling you now: I still want this, all of it. I want the tears; I want the pain. Transition doesn't have to make me happy for me to want it."

The demand for Biber's services was relentless. His *New York Times* obituary many years later would recount Trinidad pilgrimages by patients from all over the world, including three brothers who became three sisters, an eighty-four-year-old train engineer, a 250-pound linebacker, and a Native American healer, all of whom returned home as women.

"I'll tell you what it did for me," says Michelle Miles, who underwent surgery by Biber successor Marci Bowers in Trinidad in 2004 and who bought a house in the small town in 2006, leaving her New York City career to live there full-time in 2010. She now owns a downtown wine and spirits store and has served on the Trinidad City Council. "It gave me a new lease on life. I didn't walk around with the fear that my parents would die and never really know who I was. There's this shame and secrecy that comes from growing up in the fifties and sixties that just never quite leaves you until you fully embrace it. I mean, I worked on Wall Street and I had to come out to all those people. I did it, but for weeks I got phone calls. 'Hey, there's a rumor you're becoming a woman.' That was not a fun conversation to have in 2004. Was [the surgery] a panacea? No. But a new lease on life is as close to a panacea as I can hope for."

In 2012, one of Miles's friends, Muriel Vernon, a postgraduate student in anthropology at the University of California, Los Angeles, published a doctoral dissertation titled "Not Just a Guy in a Dress: Transsexual Identity, Embodiment, and Genital Reassignment Surgery in the United States." In it, Vernon describes a conversation with a male-to-female transgender patient named Lana who was just a week out of the surgical suite. She asked Lana if she felt the surgery had resolved her gender dysphoria.

"Completely," Lana replied. "I've only had the surgery for seven days, but that's exactly what it does." And then she added, "Now what I'm gonna have to recover from are the symptoms of fifty-five years of having had a penis, the fifty-five years of having been a male."

Researcher Vernon was struck by Lana's description of her previous life as an illness that surgery had cured. "Lana's candid choice to use a medicalized framework to express her thoughts on the therapeutic effects of [her surgery] provides a simple but clear insight into the ill fit between the medicalized model of gender identity disorder and the real life experience of a transsexual woman as it instantly separates body from mind, individual from society, and medicine from culture," Vernon wrote. "Lana's sense of having been 'cured' physically, yet pondering her social recovery furthermore separates notions of individual cure from those of social healing."

If the standard medical model involves recognizing a problem, diagnosing the problem, treating the problem, and curing the patient, then Vernon wondered how someone could feel "cured" of an illness that, through treatment, "changes a person so profoundly that they never return to 'pre-illness' state of 'health'. The disjuncture… illuminates the complexity of what it means to occupy a gender-nonconforming or gender-variant status."

Vernon wrote that asking the question "Does it work?" of gender-confirmation surgery patients is simply the wrong question. Rather, she wrote, it's important to ask whether surgery is intended to be an end in itself, or a means to an end: "Genitalia are so much more than body parts: they are core parts of our identity and not just fleshy apparatuses of the body machinery. The possibility of rejecting or embracing such parts of the body and the self can have profound effects on whole lives. Vaginas and penises indeed 'do' things: they permit or prevent the assumptions of kinship roles, they bestow or prohibit legal rights from marriage to custody of children, they enable or prevent intimate, sexual, or romantic relationships, they permit or prevent access to gender-segregated spaces, and so generally, they permit or prohibit participation in cultural contexts which constitute and give meaning to our everyday lives."

Genitals are not irrelevant to gender, she argued, and based on the fifty transsexual women who participated in her study, she concluded that they matter a great deal. And the same could be said of the broader culture that's clearly struggling to understand this sometimes mystifying population within the human species.

Then, of course, there's the sometimes puzzling matter of transgender sexuality. For those approaching the topic from the binary mindset, understanding the labyrinth of attraction can be like trying to decipher an ancient text that's at once unfamiliar, disorienting, and often contradictory. It sounds simple to say, "Sexual orientation is who you go to bed *with*. Gender identity is who you go to bed *as*." But that hardly explains the untidy realities on the ground.

For many years, trans men and women were either labeled as heterosexual or homosexual relative to their assigned sex at birth.[16] But trans sexuality defies such simple explanations. Some trans people may have a consistent sexual orientation throughout their lives. If they were attracted to men before their transition, they remain attracted to men. If they were attracted to women before, then they remain so afterward. Some even remain with their chosen partner during and after their transition. But don't get too comfortable with that idea, because choices in sexual partners may change, expand, or contract after transition. Sexual desire may diminish or disappear entirely.

Responses to questions posed in a National Transgender Discrimination Survey, conducted jointly by the National LGBTQ Task Force and the National Center for Transgender Equality, suggest that the range of sexuality among transgender men and woman is nearly equally distributed between those who define themselves as heterosexuals (twenty-three percent), homosexuals (twenty-three percent), bisexuals (twenty-five percent), and queer (twenty-three percent),[17] with the remaining six percent describing themselves as asexual or "other."

With less than one-fourth of transgender people identifying as heterosexual, Jack Harrison, the policy institute manager for the National LGBTQ Task Force, used those survey results to argue that trans men and women are very much a part of the LGBTQ community because so many of them identify as being on the sexual orientation spectrum. "It feels important to underscore—the overlap of trans identity and a queer sexual orientation runs deep," Harrison wrote in an essay on the Task Force website. "So, if you're ever asked why our two communities appear at times intertwined, it's because most trans people are also LGBQ. And so, united we stand."

Consider the topic settled? Don't. Claudine Griggs also says that the transition period is a dynamic process during which transsexuals go through not only physical changes, but social ones as well. They often approach that critical crossroads in their lives with a set of assumptions and expectations that may or may not turn out to be true. A man transitioning into a woman may assume that, as a woman, she'll pursue heterosexual relationships with men after her transition. Similarly, a female who transitions into a male may assume their future relationships will be with women.

But once equipped with new genitalia, reality sets in. New and perhaps unimagined sexual possibilities present themselves. Limitations emerge. Experimentation begins. Expectations change.

"I thought I would emerge from transition as a quasi-June Cleaver," Griggs says. "However, I soon discovered that society would not let me become June Cleaver even if I wanted, and after a while, I didn't want to be that kind of woman."

And, as the saying goes, it also takes two to tango. Pursuing the sexual life they imagined sometimes can run aground because desired partners may not accept or be comfortable with the idea of being sexually involved with someone who has undergone such a dramatic change.

"Many hetero men or their families reject male-to-female transsexuals outright, which limits developing relationships and heterosexual expressions," Griggs says. "Same with female-to-males, although my experience suggests it's much easier for them to find a 'wife' than it is for a male-to-female to find a 'husband' in any traditional sense."

Griggs often compares those situations to inmates trapped in a same-sex prison for long periods of time. For some, homosexual sex is better than no sex at all, and rationalizations are made. "Transsexuals have to accommodate their desires in conjunction with the real-world possibilities," she says. "The possible can deform the desired."

8

Coming Out in Trinidad

In 1969, when Stanley Biber first consulted a more experienced Johns Hopkins surgeon about a procedure now commonly known as a "vaginoplasty"—and then performed one on an acquaintance who'd sought his help—he quickly recognized that he'd created for himself a whole new set of problems in Trinidad: How to explain all this to the Sisters of Charity who were still helping run the hospital where he worked, and to the mostly Roman Catholic community that, in time, would be hosting about three transgender medical pilgrims a week, often with friends, lovers, and family in tow.

At first Biber kept the charts of his early transgender surgery patients in the hospital administrator's safe. Claudine Griggs says she once saw a television interview with one of Biber's "earlier wives" who said the surgeon even concocted a cover story about his first gender confirmation surgery patient being "an accident victim" to avoid raising questions among his bosses.

But as word got around, more and more patients began traveling to Trinidad for the surgery. "Obviously when they started having a lot of 'accidents,' they knew something was going on," Griggs says. Besides, secrets don't stay secret for long in a town the size of Trinidad, especially with so many strangers wandering around. Biber recalled to Ray Herst, the editor of Trinidad's *Chronicle-News,* that he gradually became aware that "gossip" about him was circulating among the locals. During that conversation in April 1973, just three years after doing his first gender confirmation surgery, Biber heard that someone in town was distributing copies of an article about one of his patients whose transition story appeared in a newspaper in Washington state.

"So long as they are being distributed, I'm pretty firm in my mind that we should admit that we are doing this type of surgery, which is completely legal and completely necessary," he told Herst. He also corrected the estimated $10,000 cost of the surgery mentioned in the article.

"There are certain types of these patients who have been taken advantage of for years by the tremendous money value, or price, that has been placed on the operation by certain groups in other areas," Biber said, offering no specifics. "We don't want to do that…. That is why we do the job for these patients for the minimum figure of $1,000."

Biber eventually explained to his bosses what he was doing, and then reached out to local religious leaders and others in the community to explain that he was doing the surgeries out of a sense of compassion, and without making a moral judgment about the individuals who sought him out. He saw them as people in pain and himself as having the power to relieve that pain. His decision to directly address local skeptics and critics was, he told a Denver reporter in 1998, "one of the smartest things I've ever done."

Griggs says she'd once heard that one of the Sisters of Charity at Mt. San Rafael Hospital had written to the Vatican for guidance shortly after Biber began doing the surgeries. What were the nuns to do when dealing with patients whose elective surgery involved tinkering with God's flesh-and-blood handiwork? "And they got a response back," Griggs says, recalling the story she had heard. "It wasn't from the Pope, but from somebody there, who said, 'Just keep doing your work.'"

That story is both supported and contradicted by notes from researchers Elizabeth Bucar and Anne Enke, who in a 2011 article in the academic journal *Feminist Studies* titled "Unlikely Sex Change Capitals of the World: Trinidad, United States, and Tehran, Iran, as Twin Yardsticks of Homonormative Liberalism," wrote: "The claim that the Vatican 'gave its blessing' or a 'special dispensation' to Biber to conduct SRS circulates widely as lore and fact. However, no documentary evidence has ever been provided to prove it, and no other national newspaper has been willing to repeat it as fact. It appears most likely that at the time (early 1970s) the Vatican did not rule against the practice, which is not quite the same thing as a blessing."

The two researchers also noted that, although the Vatican does not have an official position on gender confirmation surgery, some reports suggest it apparently did circulate a Catholic theological perspective in 2000, and then again in 2002, to the presidents of bishops' conferences claiming that the surgeries are "merely superficial and external and not able to change the sex or gender of the individual: if she was born a female, she remains female; if he was born a male, he remains male." In January 2015, Pope Francis met with Diego Neria Lejarraga, who was born as a girl in Spain and raised as a devout Catholic before transitioning to male. The Vatican did not confirm the private meeting, but if true, it was considered a first for a sitting pope.

Regardless, by the time Griggs showed up for her surgery in 1991, she says Biber and the hospital staff were welcoming wary transgender patients in a way that affirmed their dignity and reassured the patients about the professionalism of the surgeon and the hospital staff. "I couldn't understand why the sisters were looking over me while I was in the hospital and making sure transsexuals weren't mistreated, and coming in to see us and checking on us," Griggs says. "It never made sense to me, but I was grateful."

But how did we get from that uncertain start to the current cultural crossroads where, suddenly, transgender stories seem to be *everywhere*? The modern big bang, of course, was *Vanity Fair*'s decision to feature a glammed-up Caitlyn Jenner on its June 2015 cover. The photograph, shot by fabled celebrity photographer Annie Leibovitz, showed the 1976 Olympic men's decathlon champion post-transition with shoulder-length brunette tresses, hormonally developed breasts, and wearing a cream-colored strapless bodysuit—a cover the American Society of Magazine Editors later named its cover of the year. That feature laid the groundwork for an E! Network reality TV show called *I Am Cait* that, although short-lived, debuted on July 26, 2015, and chronicled Jenner's post-transition life.

In May 2016, *Time* magazine writer Charlotte Alter published an eye-opening piece called "What Trans Men See That Women Don't" which spotlit an often overlooked population within the transgender community—genetic females who transition into life as a male, whether with or without surgery. Based on interviews with nearly two dozen trans men and activists, Alter's story revealed persistent cultural sexism and fascinating differences in the way men who were raised and socialized as female were treated differently once they presented themselves to the world as men, especially at work. "As soon as they came out as men," Alter wrote, "they found their missteps minimized and their successes amplified. Often, they say, their words carried more weight: They seemed to gain authority and professional respect overnight."

Then, in January 2017, *National Geographic* released a special issue titled "Gender Revolution" featuring a photo of a pink-haired adolescent transgender girl and the quote: "The best thing about being a girl is, now I don't have to pretend to be a boy." About the same time, former NBC and CBS news anchor Katie Couric hosted a spin-off two-hour documentary aired during prime time on the National Geographic Channel that included interviews with sex and gender experts, trans men and women, and college students whose identities go beyond binary gender roles.

The months that followed brought a cascade of transgender issues in the news, from ongoing debates about public restrooms, to President Donald Trump's announcement in July 2017 of his plan to ban transgender people from military service, to the ensuing court battles over that decision, to the release a few months later of a report by the Human Rights Campaign Foundation (in conjunction with the Trans People of Color Coalition) which concluded that at least twenty-five transgender people were killed in the US the previous year, making it the deadliest year for them in at least a decade. It also concluded that since 2008 more than 2,300 transgender and gender-diverse people had been killed worldwide, most of them under the age of thirty.

That report profiled and featured photographs of each of the US victims, and ascribed the increase in violence to "anti-LGBTQ prejudice, racism, too-easy access to guns, and increasing political attacks on the transgender community at both the state and federal level." It also unambiguously concluded that things had gotten worse since Trump's election in 2016. The title of that report, "A Time To Act," sounds like a call to arms, and its boldface opening paragraph wastes no time in pointing the finger of blame: "In 2017, when the flames of hate and discrimination are fanned by those at the very highest levels of government, the consequences can be deadly."

But what might have seemed like an explosion of transgender awareness in American culture was deceiving. A slow wave had been building since World War II and began to crest in the 1990s. When that wave finally broke with that 2015 *Vanity Fair* cover, many Americans—though not anyone who'd been paying attention—felt like they'd been caught unawares. How different, really, was the Jenner experience from that of Christine Jorgensen, who more than six decades earlier made international headlines—and inspired Walt Heyer—by doing pretty much the same thing? In the updated 2017 edition of *Transgender History*, Susan Stryker called Jorgensen's decision to undergo surgery and her subsequent fame "a watershed event" that "brought an unprecedented level of public awareness to transgender issues, and helped define the terms that would structure identity politics in the decades ahead."

Stanley Biber, of course, had been talking about the presence of transsexuals in society for years. "Are any of you into mythology?" Biber asked a gathering of mostly transgender men and women at the New Jersey Medical Center in 1997. "If you read some of the Greek mythology, you'll remember reading about the goddess Venus Castina responding with sympathy to the yearning of feminine souls locked up in male bodies."

During that talk, a variation of his standard stump speech, he recounted other instances of apparent transsexualism from classical history, including the Renaissance tale of King Henry III of France who he said dressed as a woman, and by royal decree was to be considered a woman "even when he went into the House of Delegates" where he was addressed as "Her Majesty."

Biber told of one Roman emperor who "married a powerful slave and took up the tasks of wife and ... offered one half of the Roman Empire to the physician who could equip him with female genitalia." From behind wire-rimmed gold glasses whose thick lenses magnified his eyes, Biber paused before smiling and delivering his punchline: "Too bad I wasn't born in those days. Instead of ranching in Colorado, I could've ranched half of Italy or maybe the half of the Mediterranean."

9

Claudine Awakens

On the day of her scheduled surgery, Claudine Griggs was coaxed from sleep by the gentle urgings of an unfamiliar voice in her room in Trinidad's Mt. San Rafael Hospital: "It's 5:50 a.m. Time to get up and shower. Time to get ready for your operation. Today is your day."

This is it, she remembers thinking, *the day I've dreamed of for seventeen years, the day I've suffered and struggled for, the day I'm convinced was fated for me on July 27, 1953, when I entered this world two months premature and the doctor erroneously proclaimed, "It's a boy!"*

She felt oddly, unexpectedly, at ease as hospital staffers prepped her for surgery. Still afraid, for sure, but confident in her decision and confident in Stanley Biber—and that was before a nurse administered a shot of muscle relaxant. Once the shot was given, she bade farewell and exchanged "I love yous" with Carolyn, the companion and lover who'd traveled with her to Trinidad, and with help moved from her hospital bed onto a bedside gurney, feeling "invincibly secure." She drifted into twilight as she was wheeled into the operating room, her last thought rising like a bubble before she drifted off to sleep: *If I die on this table, please be sure to thank everyone for at least trying to help me.*

Around 2 p.m., Griggs awakened again, this time aware of intense pain and struggling to make sense of the moment. She imagined it felt something like childbirth, and she felt strangely...normal, not at all the mis-bodied freak she had always felt herself to be. Had she been taken to the maternity ward by mistake?

She awoke again about an hour later, noticing for the first time a box of sanitary napkins on the windowsill next to her bed. She was coming to, and things were getting clearer. She understood then that she was not delivering a child, that the previous sensation of labor was just a "beautiful dream" about being a woman. She realized for the first time that her pain was surgical. That led her to another realization: Although physically transformed, she remained a transsexual woman.

As the minutes unspooled in that foggy anesthetic dawn, she saw something else, something she hadn't noticed before: two bouquets of flowers on the windowsill. And Carolyn was there, sitting next to the bed. She explained that Griggs's coworkers at both her current and previous jobs had sent her flowers. Griggs drifted in and out, and by 5 p.m. she was vomiting violently, heaving the fluids in her stomach into a small plastic tray, each time feeling a convulsive agony as she strained her many stitches.

Still, around 6:30, she summoned the energy to peek beneath her blankets and sheets. Though it was hard to lift her head, she saw sanitary napkins between her legs, secured by some sort of belt around her waist. Catheter tubes snaked from beneath the pads. Her abdomen was bruised and swollen—the results of what she considers a "benevolent assault." All in all, the frightening landscape of her body was one of orderly devastation. She thought, *I guess this was real after all.*

After struggling through pain and nausea during the first twenty-four hours following surgery, Griggs was conscious enough by about noon the following day to understand the news Carolyn brought: Two of their friends were driving from Denver to spend the weekend in Trinidad. They were the kind of irreverent friends who sent Griggs a get-well card featuring a colorful rooster in a surgeon's mask—the message inside read: "Dr. Pecker—Wishing You Well." Griggs was excited, but confessed later to being apprehensive about the idea that "friends are coming to visit me on the transsexual ward of a transsexual hospital in a transsexual town; I hate it, but am determined to face them and smile and tell them how fine everything is and how I haven't any concern about the surgery and am sure life will henceforth be grand, glossing over my real feelings with the resolute and stoic residue from a past existence."

During the groggy days that followed, she recalls regular visitations from one person in particular, one of the Sisters of Charity. In the memoir Griggs would eventually write, she would call her Sister Antonia Carmen. In fact, her name was Sister Roberta Marie, and her official role at Mt. San Rafael was "patient representative." The recovering Griggs remembers her no-nonsense commitment to making sure surgeon Stanley Biber's transgender patients were treated gently and with compassion. The nun became a sort of recurring apparition that would remain with Griggs in the months and years ahead.

"She was aged, probably mid- to late-seventies. It's hard to guess given my state of mind at that point," Griggs recalls. "But she was tough, and she made it very, very clear that if there was any hint of mistreatment that she was to be notified. And I think she was absolutely sincere. I don't think for her it was a job. It was her mission .... To find people who could know that part of my life and still treat me as a human being, that was remarkable to me."

————————

On the third day after her surgery, Dr. Biber and two nurses entered the room Griggs shared with another of his post-surgical transgender patients. He first examined the roommate, who had her surgery a day after Griggs. Hers was a bit more complicated, because she also had breast implants done at the same time. The surgeon concluded that she was healing well, top and bottom, and is "going to look terrific in a formal."

Then he crossed the room to focus on Griggs in the adjacent bed. He gently lifted the sanitary napkins away from her crotch and seemed pleased with what he saw. Actually, more than pleased. He turned to the accompanying nurses with what

Griggs recalls as exaggerated enthusiasm. "Look at that clit, would you?" he said. "God, I did a job! She's going to have a wonderful time with that."

As jarring as that proclamation might seem, Griggs says Biber's directness, braggadocio, and swaggering self-confidence was reassuring to someone whose expectations for the surgery were strikingly low.

"I just really wanted to come out of it with a functional vagina, and to be healthy, to not have a permanent disability or somehow not recover fully," she says. "And the fact that he was so confident as a surgeon... I certainly didn't want my surgeon to come in and say 'Well, maybe it'll work, maybe it won't, maybe you'll be OK, maybe you won't.' I wanted somebody, especially at that moment when I was absolutely terrified, to say 'Don't worry. I'm really good, and I'm gonna take care of you.'"

On the day before her surgery, Biber's parting words to her had been, "Tomorrow is your day," which she took to mean, "Tomorrow my whole world is devoted to you. We're gonna take care of everything and you're gonna be fine." To hear him declare her newly fashioned clitoris so spectacular was, in the moment, a comforting boast. "All I could see were bruises," she recalls of that moment. "I just wanted to get out of there alive and have a reasonable chance at a happy life. My clitoris was completely irrelevant. But for me that was great."

One of the administrative duties that Biber assigned to his transgender patients in the days after surgery was to complete and sign a form that legally changed a patient's sex designation. It certified that Biber was licensed to practice medicine in Colorado, and that he had performed "certain surgical operations" that required the sex designation of the patient to be changed. In Griggs's case, the designation "male" would be changed to "female" as of the date of surgery, hers being July 24, 1991. By the time the form arrived in Griggs's room at Mt. San Rafael Hospital, it already had been signed by Biber and a notary public.

Even though the official declaration represented what Griggs had always believed about herself, she was bothered that the document arrived without her having been consulted, "similar to being born and having a doctor proclaiming that I am male without asking what I thought about it." But she understood its purpose. She eventually could use the affidavit to change the sex designation on her birth certificate.

She showed the document to Carolyn, who said, "Well, I guess it's official."

After all she'd gone through to get to that point, Griggs's answer—"Is it?"—seemed strangely ambivalent. Looking back, she says even then that she understood a hard reality. Although her body now conformed with the way she saw herself, she was still and would forever be a transsexual woman.

"Certainly I had been through surgery, and the affidavit was official, but I knew even then that the surgery wouldn't make much difference to many people. I was still 'officially' transsexual, and the associated prejudice still existed," she says. "That's what I think I was saying to Carolyn. The sentiment didn't really seem possible."

A few days later Griggs was freed from the catheter, the last tether holding her in the hospital bed. The nurse who liberated her by sliding the tube from her urinary tract told her she was free to climb from the bed as soon as she felt able, but with a warning that she likely would be very weak after days off her feet.

Eight days before, Griggs was running thirty miles per week. How bad could it be? She maneuvered herself into position and set her feet on the floor, triggering a tidal wave of pain between her legs. Tentatively bracing herself on the edge the bed, she stood.

Her body felt like it weighed 400 pounds, and her thighs were quaking. With the nurse alongside, she managed to take three steps toward the bathroom, turn, and take three steps back to the bed. But by the time she sat down again, she was panting. The nurse took her pulse. It was 130 beats per minute.

Griggs eased herself back into the bed, exhausted. Later she wrote in her journal: "I have regained my freedom but am too feeble to do anything with it."

Twenty-four hours before she was scheduled to leave the hospital, Griggs allowed herself to daydream. Her scheduled six days of recovery seemed to last an eternity, with regular bouts of pain, nausea, and humility. She had begun to think of leaving Trinidad as an escape from all that. As she imagined it:

> I'll not be troubled by self-doubt and gender dysphoria and insecurity; I'm going to be clean and new and fresh and unblemished; my elation over having obtained this surgery, after so desperate a struggle, will last forever; and once the gauze packing is removed from my new vagina, once my body has healed completely, I will have been cured of a terrible and cruel affliction. I am going to love myself and life and everyone I meet; I shall fit easily into society. Now I have all the answers—answers given at the hands of a skilled surgeon and the kind words of a few compassionate people.

But even then, with a better, once-unimaginable future ahead of her, she recognized that her post-op life back in Southern California was likely going to be more complicated than that. As the hour of her release neared, she found herself struggling with an irrational fear. Leaving Trinidad and Mt. San Rafael Hospital meant walking away from a place where she felt accepted and respected, where her every need was met by people who conferred on her an unfamiliar dignity.

Her route home would take her through vast stretches of

rural Arizona, New Mexico, and California. If something went wrong, she'd be in the hands of doctors who might be incompetent or even malicious. She imagined the car breaking down and winding up in some desert-town health clinic.

"To go to a strange doctor in that condition was just absolutely terrifying," she would recall years later. "I'd had bad experiences with doctors, too. I had one doctor not only refuse to treat me when I went to see him, but he told me to commit suicide. I mean, that was a doctor. If doctors were like that, you can imagine what just everyday average people were like. So I did whatever I could to stay away from people."

Once on the road west, with Carolyn at the wheel, her mind took her to ever darker places. By nightfall, as they searched for a hotel, she was convinced everyone they passed was a potential rapist or murderer, that she'd be brutalized as she was once before and left for dead on the side of the road.

But their drive also would take them through Holbrook, Arizona, past a Best Western hotel where they'd stayed on the way to Trinidad. Griggs thought back to that night, of making love to Carolyn with her male body for the last time. She recalled the experience, but remains uncertain about precisely which emotions the memory stirred. Longing? Regret? Anticipation? In any case, it seemed to her like it was a long, long time ago.

10

Laura Awakens

"Laura, Laura, can you hear me?"

After traveling to Mt. San Rafael in Trinidad as Walt Heyer, and signing in as Andrea West, Stanley Biber's newest patient had told the hospital staff during his intake interview that his preferred post-op name would be "Laura Jensen," for no particular reason. Now someone was calling that name from a distant place as he struggled back toward consciousness following his surgery.

What Laura remembers of those first conscious moments was an unfamiliar weightlessness. Wherever she was, she was fighting no battles. She had no confusion or torment, and was filled with a sense of serenity as warm as a lover's embrace.

The euphoria didn't last long. As with Claudine Griggs and countless other Biber patients, Laura Jensen was soon aware of intense pain and trying to manage the side effects of her elective assault. But according to the deceptive plan she'd developed to keep the surgery a secret from the people in her life, including her mother and her boss at Honda, there wasn't much time to pull herself back together. She'd planned to leave Trinidad only four days after surgery, not Biber's recommended six, and fly home to Southern California to recuperate. She would then proceed with the scheduled gallbladder surgery she'd used as a cover story for her two- or three-week medical leave from work.

The newly minted Laura Jensen seemed to have the same penchant for impulsive decision-making as Walt Heyer. The desire for privacy, for maintaining the secret from professional colleagues, was overriding all logic. The die was cast; she had to push herself beyond the pain in order to stay on schedule to return to the double life she planned to lead: Walt at work, Laura Jensen when not.

As scheduled, Laura visited her gallbladder surgeon a week later for pre-op preparations. The doctor was a long-time friend who knew her first as Walt Heyer, and who was aware of the long struggle that brought her to this moment. The surgeon was curious about Biber's handiwork, and after a pelvic examination, pronounced it well done. But he was also concerned that his still-weak patient wanted to proceed with a second surgery so soon after the first. The physician advised against it, feeling she was still too weak. But Laura Jensen insisted.

A friend offered Laura her home in Manhattan Beach as a refuge where she could deal with the lingering after-effects of the two surgeries, and at the time that seemed like her best option. The owner told Laura she could have the place for a week, after which Laura planned to return to work as Walt.

At times that week, Jensen felt she had finally conquered the demons who'd shaped and complicated her life. She worried about the coming ordeal of managing both her career and her new life as a woman, of course, but also felt an energizing anticipation about the future. She compared it to walking into an unfamiliar house, in total darkness. "You knew you'd be stumbling, tripping, and finding your way one little step at a time, and would not know for sure where you'd end up."

And stumble she did. The weeks and months that followed brought countless complications, some anticipated, some not. Among the people she'd told nothing about her years-long gender identity struggle was her mother, with whom she'd never had a particularly close relationship. Her mother knew nothing about her son's diagnosis of gender dysphoria, history of breast implants and hormone treatments, or the more radical recent surgery in Trinidad. "She had for most of my life been upset about almost everything I did," so telling her would be "just another upset after forty years of upsets."

At the time, her mother was dealing with some issues of her own. Retired and living on Social Security income, she was struggling to pay her rent following a recent increase.

She was on a wait list for federally subsidized housing, but nothing had yet come through. By then, Laura had resumed commuting two hours each way from her condo in inland Ontario to the office in Gardena, in the heart of the Los Angeles basin. She offered the condo rent-free to her mother, who jumped at the chance. Laura also decided to rent a place in coastal Manhattan Beach near where she'd stayed during the recuperation week. The day she moved her mother into the condo was the day she decided to tell her the truth.

It didn't go well. Amid the tears and confusion, her mother confessed that she'd always known her son was different. She also enumerated the many ways she knew about Walt's lifelong strangeness, which Laura found annoying. "I had just undergone radical treatment for gender dysphoria. I really did not need anyone, especially my mother, to elaborate on how different I was and apparently how I always had been very different."

On top of that, Laura was already having doubts. The problems she hoped the surgery would fix—aggravation, distress, depression—were still an issue. The battle that for years had raged inside her continued.

A more practical complication arose about six months after the surgery: The prospect of legally changing her name from Walter James Heyer to Laura Jensen. While she was confident she could bluff her way through her executive career as Walt and live her off-hours as Laura, she had overlooked a detail pointed out by her attorney: After gender-confirmation surgery, she could not legally continue to work as Walt. Making that unusual adjustment on the paperwork at Honda was going to out her, setting up a problem for which she had no solution. She dragged her feet for months, but eventually her attorney convinced her that it was better to tell the truth than have her bosses find out some other way.

Had she not been so focused on her own inner turmoil, Jensen might[18] have found hope in a lawsuit that was working its way through the legal system related to her rights as an employee under a section of the Civil Rights Act of 1964. In that case, Kenneth Ulane, a decorated Army combat pilot in

Vietnam, was hired as a pilot for Eastern Airlines in 1968, but was fired as Karen Frances Ulane in 1981 after undergoing hormone treatment and gender confirmation surgery. Ulane sued, claiming discrimination, and won her case in the lower courts, but in August 1984—several months after Jensen's surgery in Trinidad—the US Court of Appeals for the Seventh Circuit reversed that decision. It claimed, among other things:

> In our view, to include transsexuals within the reach of Title VII [of the Civil Right Act] far exceeds mere statutory interpretation. Congress had a narrow view of sex in mind when it passed the Civil Rights Act, and it has rejected subsequent attempts to broaden the scope of its original interpretation. For us to now hold that Title VII protects transsexuals would take us out of the realm of interpreting and reviewing and into the realm of legislating. This we must not and will not do.[19]

In October 1983, when Laura Jensen decided she could no longer avoid that difficult conversation with her boss at Honda, the original Ulane decision had not yet been reversed. But Jensen was engulfed in personal turmoil, so all of that was taking place far off her radar. Over a business meal, and presenting herself as Walt Heyer, she explained to her boss that she'd already had the surgery, and that her new name was Laura Jensen. Her stunned supervisor tried to digest the news, finally confessing: "I have no idea how to handle this. I'll need to take this to the president." In the meantime, he asked her to take a leave from work while Honda worked out a plan to manage the gender transition. She assumed there'd be complicated personnel issues beyond her own situation. How, for example, would they handle the unusual disclosure to her fellow employees?

Days led to weeks as she waited. Finally, on October 25, her forty-third birthday, her boss asked to meet her and Honda's personnel director at a local restaurant. They explained their plan:

Honda would give her six months' severance pay in return for her quietly disappearing from the company. She could never set foot on Honda property again or discuss the termination with anyone. If she didn't go along with the plan, they'd simply eliminate her position. They presented a termination agreement and asked her to sign.

She did.

The months of unsuccessful job interviews that followed convinced Laura Jensen that her high-flying executive career was over. Her physical appearance didn't help. She continued to have cosmetic surgeries—facial surgeries and skin peels in addition to ongoing hormone therapy—so she could better pass as a woman. But the war raging inside her continued as well, as did her drinking and drug use. Reeling from the financial stress of unemployment, alimony, and child support payments, she decided to downsize her lifestyle. She gave up her Manhattan Beach apartment and rented a room from what turned out to be a cocaine dealer.

What remained of her severance money began disappearing up her nose. She had to ask her mother to take over her mortgage payments on the condo. Her friends and former coworkers began avoiding her, adding social isolation to her long list of torments. One day, after a particularly vicious booze-and-cocaine binge, she called a friend who once had offered to help her get sober. The next day, she attended her first Alcoholics Anonymous meeting, arriving like someone who'd just crawled out from a Dumpster.

"I was a disgusting, messed-up sight by any standard: a half-man, half-woman smelling of vomit and body odors after a night spent sleeping outdoors," she remembers. "Beard stubble poked out in patches on my face where electrolysis still needed to be done."

Her eyes were bloodshot, and she was wearing a rabbit-fur coat that had kept her warm the night before while she slept in a

Long Beach city park. It was crusted with the former contents of her stomach. She took a seat in the back, at least thirty feet away from the others at the meeting. No one objected.

During that meeting, she met a man who offered to let her live in his unconverted garage for a while—as long as she was committed to recovery. It seemed like the best offer she was going to get, so she took it.

11

First Steps on a Long Road

If the post-op lives of Claudine Griggs and Laura Jensen seem just as complicated as their lives before their surgeries, it's because they are. And that's something often lost in conversations and cultural assumptions about surgery as a way to address gender dysphoria.[20]

Many advocates claim a "success rate" after hormone treatment and gender confirmation surgery of about ninety-seven percent. Brynn Tannehill, a US Naval Academy grad and former naval aviator who began her gender transition in 2010 and today writes for various publications about LGBTQ issues, argued that case and set out to disprove skeptics in a 2014 *Huffington Post* story headlined "Myths About Transition Regrets."

Tannehill wrote that skeptics "cite their two favorite studies, without actually looking at what the actual studies said, and drag out some old anecdotes. In short, they try to muddy the waters the way climate-change deniers or creationists do by throwing up a cloud of chaff and hoping no one will look any closer."

The first myth she references is a 2011 study titled "Long-Term Follow-Up of Transsexual Persons Undergoing Sex Reassignment Surgery: Cohort Study in Sweden," which tracked the long-term aftermath of 324 Swedes who had undergone gender confirmation surgery. Were they still alive? If not, how did they die? Had they attempted suicide? Were they otherwise mentally healthy? Did they abuse alcohol or drugs? Had they been convicted of a criminal or violent offense since their surgery?

Compared to a healthy control population, the study found substantially higher rates of overall mortality, death from cardiovascular disease and suicide, suicide attempts, and psychiatric hospitalizations in sex-reassigned transsexual individuals. It identified post-surgical transsexuals as a "risk group" that needed long-term psychiatric and follow-up care. "Even though surgery and hormonal therapy alleviates gender dysphoria, it is apparently not sufficient to remedy the high rates of morbidity and mortality found among transsexual persons," the researchers wrote. That conclusion echoed a 2006 Belgian study that concluded: "While sex reassignment treatment is an effective therapy for transsexuals, also in the long term, the postoperative transsexual remains a fragile person in some respects."

But Tannehill focused her rebuttal on the idea that post-op transgender men and women are more likely to commit suicide, claiming it "grossly misrepresents" the study's findings: "The study outright states that medical transition is supported by the other research, and the study is not intended as an argument against the availability of such treatment." In fact, the researchers wrote, previous studies "suggest that sex reassignment of transsexual persons improves quality of life and gender dysphoria." Tannehill also cited a 2009 Swedish study which found that ninety-five percent of surgically altered individuals reported positive life outcomes as a result.

Those suicide statistics? Tannehill argued that the study was based on individuals who transitioned before 1989, when health care, surgical techniques, and societal attitudes were less advanced. "It should come as no shock that as society accepts transgender people, they suffer fewer side effects of minority stress," Tannehill wrote. "This conclusion is supported by other recent studies that found that individuals who receive treatment not only are better off than those who didn't, but are not significantly different in daily functioning than the general population."

That point of view is echoed, it turns out, by the study's lead author. In 2015, trans historian and advocate Cristan Williams tracked down Dr. Cecilia Dhejne, who began working with a Stockholm gender research team in 1999. Williams asked Dhejne if the conclusions of her landmark study were being misrepresented.

"Yes! It's very frustrating!" the researcher replied. "I've even seen professors use my work to support ridiculous claims. I've often had to respond myself by commenting on articles, speaking with journalists, and talking about this problem at conferences…. People who misuse the study always omit the fact that the study clearly states that it is *not an evaluation of gender dysphoria treatment*. [Emphasis added.] If we look at the literature, we find that several recent studies conclude that [World Professional Association for Transgender Health] Standards of Care-compliant treatment decreases gender dysphoria and improves mental health."

Dhejne cited the results of a 2009 survey of available research that assessed the quality of life of people with gender identity disorder who received hormonal therapy as a part of gender confirmation surgery. That study offered a guarded conclusion: "Very low-quality evidence suggests that sex reassignment that includes hormonal interventions in individuals with Gender Identity Disorder likely improves gender dysphoria, psychological functioning and co-morbidities, sexual function, and overall quality of life."

"Of course trans medical and psychological care is efficacious," Dhejne told Williams. "[That analysis], confirmed by studies thereafter, shows that medical gender confirming interventions reduce gender dysphoria."

Tannehill also blasted the notion, based on a 2004 British study, that concluded gender-confirmation surgery isn't effective—another "gross misrepresentation" of the research, she claimed—and the idea that many who undergo the surgery later regret it. She cited studies that put the level of post-op regret at between one and four percent—about the same as people who later regret having gastric banding surgery to lose weight. More recently, the European Association of Urology developed a transgender-specific questionnaire to gauge the quality of life of post-surgical transgender men and women, and in March 2018 concluded for the first time that "gender surgery significantly improves quality of life for the majority of patients." The study shows that eighty percent of male-to-female patients perceived themselves as women post-surgery—even while pointing out that the quality of life of transgender individuals is still significantly lower than the general population.

But like many shouting across the gender and cultural divides, Tannehill picked her battles carefully. She downplayed the suicide findings of the Swedish study and chose not to mention a January 2014 study by the American Foundation for Suicide Prevention and the UCLA School of Law's Williams Institute. It covered transgender men and women in general, not specifically those who have had gender confirmation surgery, but did begin with a rather grim executive summary:

> The prevalence of suicide attempts among respondents to the National Transgender Discrimination Survey, conducted by the National Gay and Lesbian Task Force and National Center for Transgender Equality, is 41 percent, which vastly exceeds the 4.6 percent of the overall US population who report a lifetime suicide attempt, and is also higher than the 10–20 percent of lesbian, gay, and bisexual adults who report ever attempting suicide. Much remains to be learned about underlying factors and which groups within the diverse population of transgender and gender nonconforming people are most at risk.

But the Williams Institute also concluded in a 2019 study that those who wanted and received hormone therapy and/or surgical care had considered or tried suicide "substantially" less often than those who did not receive such care—a drop from 9 percent to 5 percent.

Data massage and contradictory fact hurling has become an unfortunate American art form in this increasingly polarized era. To one extent or another, we all filter reality through the lens of our choosing. But this particular debate quickly dissolves into an incomprehensible and hostile back-and-forth. For example, in reviewing a February 2018 book by Ryan T. Anderson, *When Harry Became Sally*, Zack Ford, the LGBTQ issues editor at the progressive online news site ThinkProgress.org, accused the conservative author of similar sins of omission: "Convinced that transitioning is bad but unable to offer any alternative, Anderson is left with the task of sowing as much doubt as possible about its benefits. For the most part, he regurgitates much of the non-peer-reviewed analysis that ... claims there are myriad negative outcomes for transitioning and has been widely debunked for its omissions and biases."

Ford also slammed Anderson's choice of experts, claiming many are "affiliated with the American College of Pediatricians (ACPeds), an anti-LGBTQ hate group that masquerades as a professional organization so that it can peddle anti-LGBTQ junk science. The Society for Adolescent Health and Medicine recently rebuked an article by ACPeds president Michelle Cretella for its "medical omissions, circumstantial facts, hateful interpretation, and peripheral context."

And so the debates rage. Stanley Biber attempted to decipher an answer by trying to track his post-op patients. Part of the protocol for being his patient was to complete a comprehensive survey form six months after surgery updating him on their physical, psychological, and emotional recovery. He not only wanted to know if they were satisfied with his work, but if the surgeries helped them lead happier lives. It read, oddly, like a customer satisfaction survey for purchasers of brand new genitalia. Among the requests and questions he posed to male-to-female patients such as Claudine Griggs and Laura Jensen were the following:

- Describe physical aspects of your new vagina.
- Is there satisfactory intercourse?
- Is there orgasm?
- Is there pain on usage?
- Please make a short statement as to personal
    satisfaction or dissatisfaction with your new vagina.
- Are things different for you now from the way
    they were before surgery regarding friends,
    professional relationships, with merchants?
- Has your income increased or decreased since surgery?
- Have you established some new goals since surgery?

- Did you experience any complications after
  returning home? Physically? Psychologically?
- In what ways has your life since surgery been
  different from what you had expected it to be?
- Have you married?
- Do you still think surgery was the
  correct choice for you?

Unfortunately, many of Biber's patients simply wanted to get on with their lives and stop being considered transgender. They simply wanted to disappear. So their record of completing those surveys was spotty. Or as Biber once explained, "A lot of them get married and have families and don't want to remember their lives before."[21]

But at that point the surgeon had tracked more than five hundred patients over a ten-year period. He concluded: "We're changing their bodies to match their gender identities. We're helping them feel good about themselves. I find them to be excellent citizens. I know 3,500 people who would agree."

Before you dismiss Biber's boast as hyperbole, consider the unpublished, independent case-history survey of Biber's patients conducted by Marsha Botzer, founder of Seattle's renown Ingersoll Gender Center, and a fellow researcher to whom Biber had granted access to his records. Botzer had gone back to school to earn her master's degree in counseling psychology so she could write credible letters of support for Ingersoll clients seeking surgical relief. Because some of the respondents knew she was a transgender woman, Botzer says she trusted as honest the responses they offered about their follow-up surveys of Biber's patients.

References to that study—which Botzer says she and her fellow researcher presented at a WPATH conference in Germany in about 1995—cited two hundred case histories conducted anonymously by the Ingersoll center and an "embarrassingly positive" ninety-three percent satisfaction with Biber's surgical work. One 1998 reference found a ninety-seven percent approval rating among four hundred of Biber's male-to-female patients.

"Anything that allows you to own yourself, to be yourself, and to feel solid and strong in that concept of self usually leads to a kind of freedom that goes in many directions," Botzer says. "The whole point of it is profound happiness."

She told a reporter at the time that Biber is "one of those who have done a lot of the research necessary to make the surgeries as good as they can be. In all those years, he's rendered good service. He has helped people get their lives in order."

We could leave the discussion there and not risk alienating people who embrace the prevailing opinion that transitioning through hormones and/or surgery is the right solution for most transgender people. But to do so would overlook the subtleties that shed light on some far more complicated and interesting aspects of the experience.

Griggs has always been practical and blunt about her expectations, both before and after her surgery, once writing, "I am not an advocate of sex change procedures. I know that sex reassignment is necessary for some individuals with gender dysphoria in much the same way as a radical mastectomy is necessary for some individuals with breast cancer, but I hope that such treatment is undertaken only when no other prescription exists. The best recommendation, though pointless, is don't get cancer and don't be transsexual."

One evening during the two-day drive back home to Southern California, before drifting into a heavily medicated sleep, Griggs lay awake cursing the years of suffering her body had inflicted upon her. Shouldn't her thirty-eight-year war between her gender and her physical body be over now that the surgery was done?

She compared the transition experience to the unusual talents of the Cheshire Cat in Lewis Carroll's *Alice's Adventures in Wonderland*, a creature capable, as Carroll wrote, of disappearing "quite slowly beginning with the end of the tail, and ending with the grin, which remained some time after the rest of it had gone." Griggs lamented that transsexuals like her "cannot fade gently from one sex into the other, but I have found no similar perceptual middle ground between male and female as may exist between visibility and invisibility."

The road ahead promised still more struggle, both physical and cultural. Her attitude once had been that the removal of her penis and testicles and the installation of Biber's "new vagina" would immediately and automatically bestow femininity, a process she once described as "building the mannequin to fit the dress." But in time, she says she better understood the concept of "attributed gender"—other people's unconscious evaluation of her based on cues such as physical appearance, clothing, and behavior. Some of that she could control, but not all of it. Attributed gender is "a handshake contract between observer and observed [which] cannot be enforced by genital surgery."

Griggs also draws a bright line between gender identity and gender role. "Gender identity exists independent of sanction by others or self, but gender role is codependent on both. The grave decision to act on the body is contingent on some expectation of an improved condition, even if that expectation may be realistically limited."

But all of those insights would come later, long after she rose uncertainly from her bed at Trinidad's Mt. San Rafael Hospital and took her first difficult steps into the next phase of a still-challenging reality.

12

An Uncured Life

Claudine Griggs's journey in the months following her 1991 surgery was like moving barefoot across a floor littered with Lego pieces. Even as she stepped cautiously and moved slowly, once in a while she'd find herself devastated or in tears, recoiling at some sharp, unanticipated pain.

She hadn't told her parents so many things about her life, for example, including the reason she'd been discharged from the Air Force. She'd certainly never told them she was having gender confirmation surgery, though by then they'd been aware that their son had been living as a woman for seventeen years. Not that they approved; they hadn't from the very beginning when, in late April 1974, Griggs flew from California to her parents' new home on the Florida panhandle to break the news that she was transgender and intended to transition into life as a woman. "I thought it was the decent thing to do," she recalls.

She'd tried for years to pretend she was male, even though she'd told friends as early as first grade that she thought she was a girl. She'd also once asked her mother if she'd been somehow injured or undergone some sort of operation as a baby because she couldn't understand why she felt so different from boys her age. She says her dumbstruck mother looked at her in a way that made it clear that even asking such a question was unacceptable. It was the closest they ever came to discussing her gender identity, at least until the Florida visit—which went about as badly as it could have gone.

"I should have just told them over the phone, because they just attacked me in every possible way," she recalls. "They wanted to have me confined to a mental institution. My *parents* told me to please commit suicide and save the family the embarrassment of doing this. They were threatening to sue any doctor that worked with me."

Griggs later wondered if their suggestion that she kill herself was unusual and extreme. She has since decided that, while extreme, it was not unusual. "I think that was true of a lot of people in the gay and lesbian community who were completely disowned by family members back in the sixties and seventies. I don't think it was an exclusively trans phenomenon."

Later they'd told her that if she went ahead with the surgery, they'd prefer not to know, though at one point her mother had confided, away from her father, that she *did* want to know if Claudine underwent the operation so she could be at the hospital to help. There was still the promise of a relationship there— Griggs keeps a photograph of them beaming beside her when she graduated from college as a young woman—but one built on a fragile foundation of truths never spoken.

When they visited about a month after her return from Trinidad and asked why she was not working, Griggs continued the deceit. She told them the partial truth that she was simply anemic in order to honor their wish that nothing more be said about her transition.

Griggs still wonders if that decision was the right one. How might the Trinidad experience have been different if she had allowed her mother to be there? How might that shared ordeal have helped heal the relationship between herself and her parents? "These are questions that will never be answered," she wrote in her journal at the time. "The tragedy is that they are asked."

Her cautious footfalls found other unexpected Legos. About three months after her surgery, for example, she arrived home from work to find a letter from the Department of Health for the State of Tennessee where she'd been born. She had written state officials asking about the process of amending her birth certificate to reflect her new name and gender identity. The response letter informed her that, at least in that Bible Belt jurisdiction, state law specified that "the sex of an individual will not be changed on the original certificate of birth as a result of sex change surgery."

She cried for an hour, then resolved to never again waste any emotional energy on the intransigence of the Tennessee legislature. And yet, within months she would write another letter, this one to the Los Angeles office of the American Civil Liberties Union, asking if the Tennessee law was worth challenging since many states, including California, allowed transgender people to change their birth records after surgery. She later sent an identical letter to the ACLU chapter in Nashville. She cried again a few months later when someone from the Tennessee office replied: "I regret that we cannot be of assistance to you."

By then, she had begun channeling her thoughts and anger into the journal that became *Journal of a Sex Change: Passage Through Trinidad*. In time she would write this: "Still, if I had the power to erase all knowledge of my past from the world, from the minds of my closest friends, from the legal record books, and from my own mind as well, I would do it without hesitation. I live my life grudgingly from day to day, bearing but never accepting that I am transsexual and always will be. Intermittently, a fantasy occurs: perhaps I can move to a new city, a new state, and start a life where I will never have to acknowledge (even to myself) that I am what I was."

When Claudine Griggs sat down on February 7, 1992, six months after her surgery, to complete Stanley Biber's follow-up survey, she displayed no trace of bitterness in her written comments, just resignation and resolve to make the best of her new life.

She reported that she was healing well, continuing to dilate her new vagina four times a day with diminishing pain and bleeding. Responding to the question about whether she had had satisfactory intercourse, she said she had not yet tried it. "I do not believe, even if I were inclined to attempt to intercourse, that my vagina is functional at this time," she wrote. "There is still too much pain and bleeding for me to feel comfortable even trying intercourse, and my vagina itself is still rather small (maximum depth on dilating is 4 inches, and it has only been recently that I have been able to use the larger dilator that I was provided at the hospital). Still, I am optimistic."

She had not achieved orgasm by stimulating herself either, she wrote, but reported that she had two terrific dreams during which she did achieve orgasms strong enough that they roused her from sleep. "So I assume orgasm will be possible during intercourse or masturbation, but that I need to heal a little more and learn how to work this new body of mine."

She told Biber that relationships with friends carried on pretty much unchanged, since most of them already knew her as a woman; it was much the same with merchants and people she had met during passing moments. For years, long before surgery, most people didn't know she was a transsexual woman unless she told them. Her professional colleagues had always known her as a woman, too, and she had noticed that since the surgery some of them seemed overly polite, "as if they were afraid of hurting my feelings or asking the wrong questions or saying something which they might otherwise consider innocuous." But she wrote that even that had begun to fade. She considered herself as productive as ever, working between sixty and seventy hours per week, and her income remained about the same. But, she wrote, she would trade that for "the contentment of a deliberately middle-class housewife with three kids and an IQ of 102."

As for establishing new goals since her surgery, Griggs listed three. She wanted to 1) run a marathon; 2) continue her graduate studies, perhaps a doctoral program in English, or law school; and 3) continue her work as a freelance writer.

Life with Carolyn, her lover of five years, was changing, though. They had not resumed their sexual relationship, though Griggs hoped to do so soon. She told Biber she sensed a shift in Carolyn's attitude. Her partner seemed more assertive and aggressive about what she wanted, and less pleased by Griggs. She wondered if Carolyn was trying to take a more dominant place in what before surgery had been an equal relationship. "I don't know where this partnership is headed, and I am surprised that surgery seems to have had an effect on it."

If that relationship failed, Griggs wrote, she likely would look for a male partner, though at times she says the chances of finding a satisfying love relationship of that nature, or of any nature, seemed remote.

She was also careful to explain that she did not feel the operation "cured" her, adding, "I accept the surgery as a great improvement." Still: "One thing that surgery does is solidify the realization that there is essentially no cure for transsexualism; it is a disorder that can be treated, but there is no procedure possible to make me a natural female. I will never be the person I envision I would have been if I had been born female; I can never return to 1953 and start life again; I can never have the childhood of a little girl, the adolescence of a young woman, the family experience of a young bride, wife, mother; I can never have a social history undivided by the change of life from a man to a woman."

Perhaps most distressingly, she was undergoing one of her worst depressions in many years, and expressed some disappointment that her post-op[22] life was not significantly better than her life before Trinidad.

"I expected to be happier than I am," she wrote.

She added that she did not feel particularly more feminine than before surgery, even if she liked her altered body more than she once did. She worried less about being outed as a transsexual woman. All things considered, she wrote that she would have the surgery again without hesitation. But the depression? No. That had endured through the transition. She held out hope that it would diminish over time. And if she died tomorrow, she wrote, she would be glad to die as a woman.

She concluded that while she didn't know what the future might hold for her, surgery was—for her—the right choice.

13

Relapse

If Laura Jensen's life as Walt Heyer leading up to her surgery was one of persistent lying and denial, the next leg of her journey began with an earnest commitment to recovery as part of a twelve-step program. And in that environment, surrounded by people whose lives were almost as messy as hers, she felt like less of an outcast.

Jensen recalls one particular couple from her recovery group as having an enormous impact on her. One partner, a former member of the US Army Special Forces, also known as the Green Berets, had been a tall, muscular man before transitioning into a female. His petite wife had transitioned as well, but from a female into a male. Jensen found the resulting couple alarming—"the tallest most muscular woman and the smallest most petite man ever to walk the earth. The AA meeting resembled a freak show and I was just one of the many sideshows."

She found that strangely comforting at the time. Still, her financial problems continued. While living in a friend's garage, she picked up odd jobs, including work with someone she'd met in recovery who operated a catering business. Others from that world, trying to give her a chance, hired her to clean their houses. But she was unable to pay her court-ordered alimony and child support payments, and her former wife cut off her right to visit with their children. Only her relationship with their son had survived the divorce and her transition into life as a woman, isolating her further from the life she once knew. Her mother was still waitlisted for federal senior housing, and she agreed to take over her monthly mortgage payments while Jensen moved in with a friend's mother in Alhambra, about an hour away.

As it turned out, though, the odd couple from her recovery group lived in the same neighborhood to which she moved. Initially glad to have AA friends nearby, Jensen now sees their proximity as offering her a chance to see other people living a transgender life. Through them, she could see herself more clearly —and she wasn't particularly pleased with what she saw. It was more than just a gender thing. About six months after entering recovery, Jensen recalls, the former Green Beret invited her to coffee after having a disagreement with her spouse. Thinking it her AA duty to stay with a troubled friend, she agreed. But instead of heading for a local coffeehouse, her neighbor drove them to a local bar.

Jensen's reaction was almost visceral, especially after watching her new friend order a drink and buy cocaine from the bartender. "Being in that bar felt like a living hell," Jensen recalls. "The darkened room, the burning cigarettes leaving a smoky haze that shadowed people moving about. Bars have their own special smell. The dirty carpet, the smoke and smell of spilled drinks ... I was in the process of relapse and I had not even taken a drink."

After deciding not to rat out her friend to their AA sponsors, she felt herself being pulled down, the spiral compounded by her willingness to withhold the whole truth from the people who were helping her with her own recovery. A week later, she found herself back in the same bar, having a drink and buying coke from the bartender.

———

The ever-mercurial Jensen began to wonder if having gender confirmation surgery in Trinidad was compounding her problems rather than solving them. She didn't remember anyone offering alternatives to hormone therapy and surgical intervention, so she had opted for the only solution recommended by her Bay Area therapist, Paul Walker. But had she settled on the proposed solution too quickly?

In time, she began to question the connection between her molestation as a child at the hands of an uncle and the torturous gender confusion that followed. During their few sessions together, Jensen says she doesn't remember Walker ever exploring that part of her early life. Even if Walker's gender dysphoria diagnosis was correct, why had he left what she considers a possible root cause of her dysphoria unexplored? "If he'd been skilled and gifted, when I told him I'd been molested he would have dug into that and what it does to gender identity," she recalled, mentioning the clinical term "comorbidity"—the simultaneous presence of two chronic diseases or conditions in a single patient.

She would think about those questions many times in the years to come, but at the point in her life when she first relapsed, about a year after being terminated from her job at Honda, Jensen was worried about more immediate questions and problems. Although she'd confessed her relapse to her AA sponsors and committed again to sober living, money was still a significant problem.

Jensen took a job at a retail chocolate store in Laguna Beach, a two-hour drive into Orange County from her place in Alhambra. In order to get there, she needed a car. After finding a used one at a dealership, she began making payments. She did well at work, but the long work hours, topped by a long commute, left her no time for AA meetings, as well as a lingering fear that she might relapse again. After talking it over with the people trying to help her, she decided to quit the chocolate store job after only a few weeks. The former high-flying car executive returned the used car to the dealership and asked that it be repossessed. Once her mother was approved for senior housing and moved out of Jensen's condo, Jensen, facing a mortgage default, asked her bank to repossess the condo as well.

She eventually applied for a hostess position at a new family-style restaurant within walking distance of the Alhambra place. After offering some inventive lies about her work experience— she told the manager she was widowed and had no prior employment—she was offered the position. At least it came with what she considered a cute hostess uniform. The job required her to smile a lot, but the smile was an effort.

"At the two-year mark since surgery, my family life was destroyed, my children devastated, my extended family in disbelief, my career eradicated and now out of reach, and the male man, Walt, torn from the function of life as a man," she later recalled in her memoir.

She often cried herself to sleep at night, depressed about her rocky relationship with her family, particularly the twenty-year-old daughter who had rejected her. She missed her terribly. She began to consider suicide—a way "to eliminate Laura Jensen and Walt at once," she would later write. At least her son still saw her, and at least he seemed to enjoy their time together. Jensen made sure to dress as a man during their once- or twice-monthly visits, even as she made plans to kill herself.

———

What happened next was either a lucky break or a miracle, depending on who is telling the story. A friend familiar with Jensen's worsening depression wondered if a different living arrangement might help Jensen find a way forward. The friend recommended that she move into the Pleasanton, California, home of Roy Thompson and his schoolteacher wife, Bonita, shared also by Roy's somewhat difficult mother, their confrontational teenage daughter, and a teen son, Jon, who'd been wheelchair-bound since being struck by a car at the age of nine. Thompson, with a doctorate degree in cross-cultural psychology and a master's in theology, worked with a ministry in San Jose that focused on street people and parolees with drug and alcohol issues.

The Thompson family agreed to take Jensen into their home near San Francisco, and Jensen recalls that the Thompsons took on the job with a refreshing mix of Christian commitment and curiosity. She recalls their interest in seeing "if the Lord could restore such a broken life" as that of a chronically depressed, substance-abusing trans woman.

As Roy Thompson would later remember it: "I opened the door and there before us was a woman in a red sweater fit snugly over her well-endowed figure, with bright red lipstick and fingernails and shoulder-length hair. 'You must be Laura!' I said, inviting her in. Thus began a journey that turned a 'a few days' into nine months and nine months into twelve more years with visits lasting months at a time. We had no precedent for this situation in other relationships, nor did we find any specific scripture to act as a road map through this minefield. We did know that we had a responsibility to love her. About this, Scriptures were clear."

One night shortly after her arrival, Jensen decided to brag to Roy's mother about her once-lofty career. She recounted her work as an associate design engineer with the Apollo space program and her various executive roles at Honda. The older woman listened intently. When Jensen was done crowing, the woman just shook her head.

"Well, if you're so smart," she said, "why did you do something so stupid?"

The chocolate store for which Jensen had briefly worked in Laguna Beach had an opening in San Francisco's Embarcadero Center in the summer of 1985, and the owner called Jensen to see if she might be interested in the position. Shortly after that, Jensen became a Bay Area commuter, taking the rails each day from Pleasanton into the city where she'd once haunted the Tenderloin's gay bars while trying out her female persona. In San Francisco, with its higher-than-average population of transgender residents, she felt like less of an outcast.

At the end of her workdays, she recalls being met at the train station by Thompson's paralyzed son, Jon, who had come to escort her home. In that comforting routine, she began to find an unfamiliar peace. "The family truly showed me God's love," she would write years later. "No matter how broken my life was, they were all going to be there every day for me .... I knew then that I was going to recover. I just did not know *how* I would ever restore such a broken life."

14

The XY Factor

Claudine Griggs's analytical mind continued to churn in the months after her gender confirmation surgery in Trinidad. Maybe she was disappointed that the closure she hoped it might bring never really came. Or maybe it was a simple matter of trying to understand herself better. But she was still looking for answers about her gender identity.

On March 21, 1992, eight months after her surgery, she asked Dr. Gerald Leve, her regular endocrinologist at UCLA, about the possibility of undergoing a chromosome analysis to find some discernible physiological cause for her gender dilemma. Might such an analysis reveal some clue in her brain that could explain the difficult hand she'd been dealt at birth?

"I needed something that said why I had a feminine gender in a male body," she says. "I wanted that. I was a math-science major in high school. I like evidence. I like to be able to point and say, 'Aha! There's the two and there's the two, and they equal four!'"

Leve told her it could certainly be done, but expressed concern that she was still trying to determine if the whole thing was somehow her fault. Transsexualism was a psychophysiological phenomenon, he told her, a mystery still buried somewhere at the intersection of the brain and the body. Someday scientists might identify some unusual variation in an individual's chromosome pattern that could begin to solve that mystery. There may even come a day, he said, when doctors can do prenatal testing to check for a predisposition toward homosexuality or transsexualism, much as they already check for hereditary anomalies such as a predisposition for breast cancer. But, he asked, are you sure you want to go down that road?

To Leve she explained, "I believe I was born transsexual. But it would make me feel better if there was something I could point to and say, 'Aha! That's what did it.'"

Leve finally agreed to prescribe a "chromosome analysis with special attention to mosaicism," and Griggs decided to have the test done at the University of California, Irvine. She scheduled it for ten days later, and asked for and was granted a full day off work.

We now know far more about the development and function of the human brain than ever before in history, but that accumulated body of knowledge pales compared to what remains unknown. For example, scientists for years have been studying the phenomenon known as somatic mosaicism—the fact that cells within an organism have different genomes. They know mosaicism exists within all brains. They also know that mutations in subsets of some brain cells can cause various rare neurodevelopment disorders. But for most people, the extent and consequences of somatic mosaicism remain largely unknown, even nearly thirty years after Leve approved the test for Griggs. Scientists continue to search for credible evidence of differences in the brains of heterosexuals and homosexuals, for example, but so far they've found nothing definitive.

Still, Griggs wanted to see if her genes might reveal "the proverbial smoking gun." The test would cost $885, which she agreed to pay herself rather than haggling with her insurance company.

She arrived for her appointment in what she considered "neutral" clothing: Levi's jeans, a shirt-style white blouse, a tan corduroy sports jacket, white running shoes, and no jewelry. Her choices were calculated. When meeting for the first time with people who knew she was transgender, she avoided overtly feminine dress to assure herself that she could pass as female without those cues. She also liked her clothing to suggest that she could be masculine, when necessary, and had found that a gender-neutral style helped put others and herself at ease. Alone with a genetic counselor, Griggs explained that she was "looking for an answer I don't think I'm going to find."

"Have you already had genital surgery?" the counselor asked.

"Yes. About ten months ago. Of course, I thought that would make me feel a lot better, too, and it didn't."

"So, it's not a magic pill, huh?"

Griggs acknowledged that the test may not bring her peace, either. "Maybe even if you do find something in my chromosomes, it may not make a difference about the way I look at myself." Taking the test is a gamble, she said, but "I want to point to a cause of my existence. I want to know who I am ... why I am."

The counselor seemed less interested in Griggs' existential dilemma than in her medical history, and explained the various genetic conditions that may surface from the simple blood test Griggs was about to undergo. The blood was soon drawn, and the counselor explained that the analysis would unfold over the next three weeks. Until then, Griggs would have to wait.

As she left the office to return to her car, though, Griggs passed two women carrying twin babies about ten months old. She assumed they were mother and daughter, with the daughter's children in tow. Both twins were sleeping, a picture of contentment. But one of them was very different from the other, with a deep cavity in the center of its face the size of a tennis ball. It was where the child's nose should be, and the eyes seemed pushed awkwardly up from the opening. The disfiguration was so bad that she knew the child's appearance would forever be an issue, even after years of reparative surgery.

And for a moment, Griggs saw her own life as a blessing rather than a curse. How could she possibly compare the misfortune of her transsexualism to the misfortune of that child?

"That sense of blessedness will last for a couple of hours, the pity for the child indefinitely," she would later recount in her journal. "Even now as I write, I say a prayer for a baby that I will never know or see again."

At work about three weeks later, Griggs's phone rang. It was the genetics counselor calling even before Griggs's endocrinologist had a chance to phone her with the test results. Griggs sensed from the caller's tone that she understood the test results might be difficult for Griggs to hear. She braced herself after assuring the counselor she was willing to hear the news by phone rather than from her doctor.

"It's pretty much as we suspected," the counselor began. "You have the XY karyotype. We found no unusual variation. And concerning the other tests your doctor wanted, we eliminated mosaicism with a ninety-five percent probability."

Translation: Griggs is and always had been a genetic male. Nothing they'd found suggested otherwise.

The painful ordeal she'd undergone in Trinidad and in the months since then had not turned her into a woman, at least genetically. And honestly, she knew it would not. But she'd held out some hope that the test might reveal some quirk in her genes, some evidence of mosaicism, to explain the dissonance she'd always felt between her body and her mind. But no. The test results denied her even that satisfaction, and the results felt like one more cruelty heaped upon a lifetime of cruelties.

Griggs hung up the phone, feeling numb. As she would later write, the test "confirmed that every cell in my body has an XY karyotype," and that now she hated every cell in her body individually, not just her body as a whole. The news made her feel nauseous, made her wish for a hot bath or shower "to wash away all traces of this thing that is me." But of course, she could not do that. "I can kill it, but I cannot cleanse it."

15

The Battle Continues

By late 1985, more than two years after her surgery in Trinidad and after losing her job at Honda, Laura Jensen was asking herself some hard questions about the choices she'd made. But unlike Claudine Griggs, she did not embrace the circumstances of her new life with the same sense of acceptance. She was feeling, instead, that she'd made a terrible mistake.

"I was realizing I was a man trapped in a woman's masquerade, a fake, a fraud, a mutilated man," she later recalled in her memoir. "I did not fit in anywhere."

At the center of her doubts were questions about how she'd been diagnosed with gender dysphoria in the first place. The clinical guidelines for surgical candidates today are known as the "Standards of Care for the Health of Transsexual, Transgender, and Gender Nonconforming People," and Paul Walker, the Bay Area therapist who first diagnosed her, had helped develop them for the organization now known as WPATH, the World Professional Association for Transgender Health. As someone without an alphabet soup of academic credentials at the end of her name, who was Jensen to question those protocols? And yet, in her case, she felt like something critical had been overlooked. The more she thought about it, the more convinced she became that having a therapist explore critical chapters from a patient's past should be part of the standard way patients like her are diagnosed. She thought, *That's really where these issues lie. The standards of care need to be written in such a way that dives into the root cause of someone wanting to change their gender identity. There are clues to these things that need to be explored.*

By then, the impact of the Thompson family's love had convinced her to consider accepting Jesus Christ as her savior. And she made a decision to live once again as a man named Walt Heyer.

Heyer also decided it was time for him to live again on his own. He moved out of the Thompson home and into an apartment in Pleasanton, vowing to stay in close contact with the family upon whose support he had come to rely.

He didn't want to go through the trauma of losing a job because of the decision to publicly detransition. Or, as he put it in his memoir, "Walt didn't want to work anywhere that Laura had worked." So he decided to quit his job at the chocolate store. Roy Thompson helped him find work at an auto body shop in Sunnyvale, and the boss there, "a Christian man with a big heart for helping people who had fallen on hard times," convinced him to start attending weekly Bible study classes.

But as with every aspect of Walt Heyer's life, what might have seemed like a simple decision to correct a "mistake" was not simple at all. At first, he felt comfortable living again as a man, albeit one with female genitalia. As Walt, the familiar turmoil about his gender identity continued. As Walt, he felt more fully aware of the sexual abuse he'd endured as a child. As Walt, he would later write, "I could see the effects of the mutilation I had inflicted on my body through numerous plastic surgeries and procedures."

That was not the case while he had been living as a woman. Laura Jensen had never been abused as a child. She seemed to laugh and enjoy life more than Walt. "Laura tormented Walt's thoughts, enticing him to switch back. I began feeling more and more fragile, slowly crumbling under the weight of wanting relief from the intense emotional pain." He was mentally exhausted from fighting with Laura for control.

His body, too, was a battlefield that bore countless scars that told the story of his ongoing torment, and the details of daily living also reflected the absurd contradictions of his life. His driver's license and birth certificate said he was female, but he now was living and working as a man. Trapped in a sort of gender purgatory, he did what he had done so many times in his tumultuous past. Walt Heyer began drinking alone in his apartment, seesawing between his two personas.

"I felt like I was being torn between two genders, yet I didn't belong in either place," he later recalled. "I was so uncomfortable in my skin that I didn't want to be Walt or Laura. I had serious issues, with severe pain."

Compounding the struggle was the agony of knowing his flailing failures were playing out in front of friends, many of whom had worked hard to help him. He remembers nights at home alone, standing in his living room wracked by a pain so intense it bent him at the waist. He had to put his hands on his knees to keep himself upright. One night, drunk and dressed as Laura Jensen, he climbed to the roof of local fast-food restaurant and began shouting his intention to kill himself.

After a night in the county jail, he had to sheepishly return to the same restaurant the next day to retrieve his car. He lost his job at the auto body shop shortly thereafter, and later was ordered by a judge into a recovery treatment program. When he showed up drunk for a session with his transgender therapist, spoiling what until then had been a good relationship, she suggested he enroll in the residential Women Recovery Association to get sober. During his interview there, the association offered him a bed and a spot in the program, but first ordered him into a gritty, forty-eight-hour detox unit. From there, he was discharged into a four-month recovery program and began attending daily AA meetings with renewed commitment.

But as Laura Jensen.[23]

During the time in recovery, Laura Jensen again felt herself drawn to the spiritual component of the Alcoholics Anonymous program. For her, the vague term "higher power" referenced in AA and other twelve-step programs led consistently back to Jesus Christ. She began attending a nearby church, where the pastor, Jeff Farrar, encouraged her to be open about her ongoing struggles with both her gender identity and her substance abuse. Farrar told her Jesus was there for her, no matter who she was.

"I was definitely uncertain and nervous when Laura walked into my office," Farrar later recounted. "After a few minutes of talking, it became apparent that Laura was more nervous than I. While her story was terribly painful, it dawned on me that from her past experience with other pastors and churches, she expected to be judged and rejected."

Farrar had no experience in dealing with transgender people, and told her so. "Frankly, I was afraid that I would do damage to her with any counsel I could come up with. I simply did not know what to say to her."

At the end of their first meeting, Jensen asked Farrar if the minister might be willing to meet regularly with her. Farrar was uncertain, at best, but felt a powerful need to encourage her. What that meant, he couldn't say at the time. He eventually agreed to continue to meet, but laid out two conditions for moving forward.

First, he told Jensen he would need to be completely honest in their discussions. "I couldn't let my ignorance and inexperience of her fragility keep me from being open with my thoughts, counsel, and questions," he recalls. "Without honesty as the basis of our relationship, I couldn't be involved with integrity."

Second, he needed to tell the church's elders about his decision to counsel Laura Jensen. He was accountable to them, and he felt it was the right thing to do. Jensen's presence in the congregation was sure to raise questions, and might even drive some of the faithful away as they learned more about the unusual and troubled woman in their midst. True, Jesus welcomed lepers, tax collectors, prostitutes, and others who were among the least of his brethren. But a woman who changed genders as often as other people change their clothes? Farrar knew there'd be fallout. But he also promised to share only as much information about her case as was necessary for the elders to understand.

His intention to do so made Jensen feel vulnerable, but Farrar assured her that his superiors were trustworthy, and that their understanding and prayers might be a powerful tool. Or at least that was his hope. The minister laid out his plan, and his limitations. He did not feel qualified to offer psychological counseling. Jensen already was seeing professionals for that. His mission, as he saw it, was to guide Jensen toward salvation by encouraging honesty before God in prayer, biblically-based decision-making, accountability in her decisions, and the freedom to accept God's grace.

Given Jensen's commitment to Jesus, though, Farrar could see no way to turn her away. He agreed to do his best. "So began one of the most important and significant relationships in my life," Farrar recalls. "Walt/Laura turned out to be a tremendous source of encouragement and model of obedience in the middle of tremendous pain."

The minister drew a bright line between a broken person and a defiant person. A broken person was someone who had failed and needed to be encouraged and lifted up. A defiant person, on the other hand, needed a firmer hand, even confrontation, in order to see a way forward. Farrar saw Jensen as broken and turning toward God for help, not defiant.

About thirty church members agreed to form a sort of safety net beneath her. Although the parishioners' names were not known to Jensen, they pledged money, prayer, and love "no matter how long it took, without judging who I should become." They told her they simply wanted her to heal, and committed to pray for her recovery and restoration every week. In return, she agreed to write a weekly letter to the group in which she would share details about the battle raging within her—"no matter how bizarre, uncomfortable, or un-Christlike they may be"— so the group could pray specifically for divine intervention in those areas.

Jensen found the weekly exercise cathartic, an outlet in which to regularly express herself about the issues with which she struggled. One of those issues was employment. She walked a razor's edge when applying for positions: Should she disclose her gender struggle to potential employers, or not? When an application asked if she had lived under any other names, should she mention Walt Heyer, or not? Failure to do so was telling a lie, and more than one interviewer considered lying on the application to be disqualifying. The jobs she did find during that period of her life were far beneath her skill and intellectual level, but she was grateful for them.

Eventually, Jensen settled on a new goal: To become a counselor for people in drug or alcohol recovery. She began taking night and weekend classes at a Cupertino extension campus of the University of California, Santa Cruz, and within a year had finished her first-year classes even as she worked a job in the city and kept up with her church and AA commitments. But her second-year classes required a deeper commitment, and her fragile stability began to wobble. She began cycling back and forth between Laura and Walt, often changing from female clothes into male clothes in her car while commuting between her various obligations.

She also began noticing other differences between the two personas. Laura preferred healthy food; Walt was a junk-food fan. Walt's voice was lower, while Laura's was pitched higher. Their handwriting and opinions often were quite different. She remained Laura at school and at work, rather than risking discovery by changing whenever the impulse to do so struck. She attended men's AA groups meetings as Walt, and women's AA group meetings as Laura. The change often happened within minutes; she recalls her inconsistency as "mind-blowing."

Through it all, she understood that the key to resolving that internal battle was sobriety. Her mantra became: "Stay sober, no matter what. Stay sober."

It served her well. At the end of her two-year academic program, she graduated in 1989 with an advanced certificate in drug and alcohol studies. At 49, she was three years sober and ready to start a new career.

As Walt Heyer.

16

Finding a New State

Claudine Griggs was committed to discovering happiness in life, even if she reluctantly had to accept that hers would forever be the life of a transgender woman. For several years after her 1991 surgery in Trinidad, she'd waited for some new dawn that would leave her feeling like "I would just be me," rather than a woman born a man and then surgically sculpted into the body of a woman. It never really came. Eventually, her expectation of that new dawn faded.

"I realized I still have to go to work, I still have to eat, I still have to deal with prejudice, I still have struggles," she says. "It was not magic. [My life] was much better, and I think it got better year by year by year, simply because at some point I just had to accept that I have one life, and that life is trans, and that I'd better make the best of it."

She'd lived her life before surgery in a fortified closet. A few people knew she'd transitioned from male to female, including work colleagues and her lover Carolyn, but generally she felt that her genitalia was nobody's business but her own. Surgically removing her male genitalia, though, *had* diminished the pain of living a life in which she considered herself a misfit. In time, Stanley Biber's artfully crafted new vagina gave her the confidence to guard the closet door a little less fiercely.

I am trans, she thought. *I'm not going to stamp it on my forehead, but when it comes up and it's necessary to divulge, it's OK.*

In the first couple of years after her surgery, Griggs turned about forty or fifty pages of the personal record she'd kept about her experience undergoing gender confirmation surgery in Trinidad into a four-hundred-page manuscript that "just poured out on the page." It looked very much like a book manuscript. Eventually, she worked up the nerve to show one of her writing professors a copy.

She certainly hadn't written it with publication in mind. She'd simply wanted a record of the experience. But, she admits now, she had ambitions as a writer and, as an English major, was "infatuated" with idea of publication. Her instructor was not just enthusiastic about the manuscript, but adamant that she find a publisher.

The thought both appealed to and repelled her. Publication would represent the culmination of her writing dreams. But it also would mean crossing a cherished divide between private and public. For someone who considered privacy the central safeguard in her life, it would mean an enormous personal step.

"Biber said a lot of his patients just disappeared," Griggs says. "And a lot of psychologists said if you want to be happy you have to escape the transsexualism and just go and move and change your name and not tell anybody, except maybe your spouse—and some don't even do that. That was still something I thought about back in those days. I knew publishing the book would eliminate even the fantasy of disappearing to a new life where I could just be Claudine. And that was hard to let go of. That was one of the reasons for having the surgery, to give myself that possibility."

Even after she sent the manuscript to publishers, she remained uncertain about whether or not she was prepared for that step. But then she got an offer from North Carolina-based McFarland & Company Inc., which since 1979 had been a library-oriented publisher producing comprehensive reference works and scholarly monographs on a variety of subjects. She had a choice to make. She could go on just being Claudine, she thought, or she could publish the book and forever become Claudine the Transsexual. She held onto the book contract for three weeks before signing, struggling with the decision. During that time, her mind took her to some pretty dark places. At one point, she imagined being attacked with a baseball bat on her front porch by someone who found her gender status objectionable.

"When I got to the end of that, I was not at a very happy place," she says. "I thought, If I publish this book I will never have the opportunity to escape into a non-trans life. But then I thought, The worst that could happen is that someone will kill me, and I don't really care anyway. That was the justification I used to finally sign the contract. But there was a lot of resistance to letting that go."

McFarland quietly published the first edition of the book with the title *Passage Through Trinidad: Journal of a Surgical Sex Change* on November 1, 1995. In 2004, an academic imprint of Bloomsbury decided to flip the title and republish the book as *Journal of a Sex Change: Passage Through Trinidad*. That edition, which the publisher touted as "thoughtful and courageous," included a foreword by Judith Halberstam, a professor of literature at the University of California, San Diego, and author of *Female Masculinity*. Of Griggs's journal, Halberstam wrote: "Griggs is a startlingly accurate and self-aware diarist and her bold and truthful narrative forces the reader to turn her gaze away from the supposed oddity of the transsexual form towards the uncertainty of all gendered embodiments."

When the journal was released in November 1995, Griggs gave a copy to her employer at the time, an attorney in Irvine, California, for whom she'd worked part-time for about a year. She felt that since her secret was now out, he deserved the right to terminate her. When she gave him a copy just before she left to go home for the day, she offered to help train a new assistant if he decided to fire her.

The following morning, he greeted her with a smile and said, "Well, I bet you'd like to talk a little."

They did, and the attorney assured her that he did not want her resignation. He also cited the class she showed by telling him about the book, and said he respected her all the more for having done so.

Neither edition of her journal made her wealthy or a celebrity. But her story was suddenly part of a national and international conversation that was growing in volume and intensity year by year. There was no turning back.

Claudine Griggs wasn't imagining or exaggerating the hints of discord she felt between herself and her long-time lover Carolyn when she described them in her responses to Biber's six-month post-op survey. The relationship was unraveling, and continued to do so for about five years after their trip to Trinidad. Eventually it ended, which Griggs attributes in part to her decision to publish her journal. As she wrote in the afterword of the Bloomsbury edition, "It led to the breakup of my ten-year relationship with 'Elizabeth' [the pseudonym she used for Carolyn in the published book], which indicates that dismantling closets may not be a happy experience for everyone."

Her interactions with her parents, however, began a slow, difficult journey. While she's not sure they ever hated her, they clearly hated transsexualism. And the family problems had gone far beyond their relationship.[24] Like many parents of transgender children, they struggled first with even accepting the idea, and struggled for years afterward with the logistics of the relationship. Griggs recalls an episode in a fast-food restaurant during those years when she and her father were standing together in line. When they got their order, her father said, "Well, son, let's go." She recalls the other patrons looking around, trying to figure out to whom her father was talking.

"He was completely unaware," she says. "And, again, it's completely OK with me because I understand him. That image of me as his son is never gonna really change."

Griggs struggles with stubborn, lingering pre-transition images as well, and is easy to forgive when someone stumbles. She also apologizes when she makes the same mistake with others. "I don't think that's intentional for most people. That attribution thing is really hard to change. If a person knows someone as a man, that typically is very, very ingrained. For many parents, they'll always be a son or a daughter. And to me it's unreasonable for trans children to expect their parents to be able flip a switch, any more than a child can flip a switch and say, 'I'm not the gender I feel I am but I'm going to be the gender that matches my body.' It takes time, and it takes effort."

She doesn't see it as malicious, especially in parent-child relationships, though some might disagree. She references one particular parent whose female-to-male trans daughter, Patrick, wears a full beard and has male-pattern baldness. The parents still call him "Patti."

"These are loving parents, but they love the child that they raised," Griggs says. "They still see that child in this now fully bearded male persona that I can't see, but the parent can."

Before the 2004 edition of her journal was published, Griggs sat down to pen an afterword for the book. Her intention was to bring contemporary readers of the book up to date about her life since the journal first came out in late 1995.

By then, she wrote, American culture had evolved to the point where it seemed to be genuinely OK to be gay or lesbian. "It's almost OK to be transsexual," she wrote. "My internal transformations, prompted largely by the *Journal's* drag-her-out-of-the-closet effect, suggest that it is almost OK to be me."

She'd begun to realize that much of the pressure she felt as a trans woman was internal, rather than societal. Of course, social pressure to remain closeted was powerful and oppressive during the 1970s and 1980s, but it was less significant than her own self-disdain. Keeping her transition and surgery a secret had served an important purpose for her. She'd been able to carry on with life, working at jobs she generally enjoyed, paying her bills, passing through life as a woman with few people the wiser. But her life was in some ways unfolding by rote. She'd been focused for so long on simple survival that she'd postponed thinking much about more complicated issues such as love, marriage, children, family, and a long-term career.

But her post-op life also was increasingly marked by something unfamiliar: happiness. As the closet walls crumbled about her and she began living more openly as a trans woman, she began to see more clearly the indignities she sometimes endured were not her fault, but the fault of others.

"If a person was rude, obnoxious, demeaning, threatening, unreasonable, illogical, malicious, I didn't blame transsexualism or myself," she wrote. "I blamed the obnoxious and malicious someone.... My perspective had changed. The image of the world and my relationship to it had sharply refocused around the concept that I was not guilty."

She began to pursue her own happiness regardless of how society judged her. "Liking my physical self, or at least not hating it, somehow translated into a beginning of liking me. And it was much more interesting to approach the world each day without a perambulatory apology for my existence."

Still, she wondered if she'd made the right decision about going public. She occasionally allowed herself the luxury of fantasy. Maybe she could move to a new city or even somewhere other than California, and start life again there, far away from everything that had come before.

17

Lost and Found

The Christian church in Foster City that for years had been Laura Jensen's strength and salvation remained a beacon when she began the next phase of her complicated life. Jensen had arrived in shambles. She relied heavily on fellow worshipers, who had formed an emotional safety net and prayed often for her life to be healed. They knew her only as Laura. Then one day, feeling confident, she called pastor Jeff Farrar with a request.

Would it be OK if she came to church as Walt?

While happy to hear the sudden confidence in Jensen's voice, Farrar was stumped. What might be the impact of such a public transition on Laura? On Walt? On his congregation? What were the risks and consequences if Walt later reverted to Laura? How might such a public failure complicate everything? His primary objective was to protect the troubled person at the center of the dilemma.

Farrar discussed it with others, and also thought and prayed about the impending decision. In the end, he was convinced that the best way forward was to allow Laura and Walt to show the world the change that God had wrought. "Playing it safe out of fear of reaction or failure seemed a lack of faith," the pastor recalled.

He chose an upcoming Sunday and built his sermon for that day around an introduction of Walt Heyer. On the appointed day, Farrar spoke about God's great love for sinners, focusing his talk on the biblical story of the wealthy, but diminutive tax collector Zaccheus, from the Gospel of Luke.

In the story, Jesus, who by then was becoming wellknown, was passing through Jericho on the way to Jerusalem. A crowd had gathered, and Zaccheus was unable to see Jesus through the gathered faithful and curious. He decided to climb a tree to watch the passing entourage, which is where Jesus spotted him. When Jesus did, he acknowledged Zaccheus by name and invited himself to stay the night at the tax collector's house.

This didn't go over well among the faithful, tax collectors being particularly unpopular at the time. Why would Jesus want to stay at the home of such a sinner? But Zaccheus was so overcome with joy that he immediately pledged half of everything he owned to the poor and promised to pay back fourfold anyone he might have defrauded.

The lesson: A sinner can be saved by repentance.

With that, Farrar told the congregation the remarkable story of Walt Heyer's often chaotic journey, including the abuse, the addictions, and Walt's decision to undergo gender confirmation surgery in Trinidad. It was a stem-winder of a lead-up, and he invited the gathered to share in the good news that God had brought about a major change in the trajectory of that life. At which point, he introduced Walt Heyer to an ovation from the people in the room, some of whom had been important partners in Heyer's journey. Farrar would later call it "the most dramatic acknowledgment of God's power I have ever experienced."

Walt Heyer stood up and approached the pulpit. Every eye in the church was on him, seeing for the first time a man whom until then they'd known only as a woman. Farrar stood beside him as Heyer spoke of the role of God's grace in his life. Farrar was in tears, as were many of the church's elders and congregants.

"I know it went beyond what anyone thought they would encounter in church that day," Farrar wrote in an account Heyer later published in *A Transgender's Faith*. "It went beyond what most imagined could even happen. The reason for the impact that day was that everyone knew that God had done a miraculous work."

Farrar made it clear that God's work with Walt Heyer was far from done. His cautionary words would prove prophetic. Heyer remembers that day now as the start of a three- or four-year journey that, as always seemed the case, still had many detours ahead.

———————

Seven years after his surgery, and four years sober, the newly credentialed Walt Heyer was working weekdays as a counselor at CityTeam, a nondenominational Christian nonprofit in San Jose. Its mission: To compassionately serve the poor, the homeless, and the lost by offering hot meals, shelter, life transformation programs, clothing, hygiene items, learning and career help, and Bible study.

But on weekends, Laura Jensen was still very much a part of his life. His inability to expunge his female persona baffled him, as well as his friends, his AA sponsor, and the Christian psychologists he was regularly seeing. He was flipping erratically between his male and female personas, Walt one day, Laura the next. With various therapists, he continued searching for an explanation, sifting the possibilities. Severe depression? Posttraumatic stress disorder? Schizophrenia? They all seemed to have an opinion, but none had a definitive answer.

During that time, he also revisited a Stanford specialist who'd concluded that his case of gender dysphoria was among the most extreme she had ever seen. She reaffirmed her earlier conclusion.

Then he made what would turn out to be one of his most momentous decisions since deciding to have surgery. While studying at the University of California, Santa Cruz, in 1987 or 1988—he's no longer sure which year it was—he decided to visit Paul Walker, the Bay Area psychologist who diagnosed his gender dysphoria and recommended surgery as the best option. He intended to confront Walker about the disastrous path he felt the psychologist had charted for him.

It didn't go exactly as planned. According to Heyer's account, his claim to four years of sobriety triggered an admission from Walker that he'd never expected. Walker admitted that he, too, was in a twelve-step program, and had been addicted to drugs and alcohol at the time he first met with Heyer—the unfortunate result of taking painkillers following a ski accident. He also told Heyer he had HIV.

Before he died of AIDS, Walker wrote Heyer a note that Heyer later published verbatim in his memoir. In it, Walker congratulated his former patient on his continuing sobriety, and reiterated his conclusion that therapists should first confront alcohol or substance abuse issues with their clients before attempting to address any gender issues. Walker conceded that he'd not done so in Heyer's case, and assured him "that I share, as best I can, some of the pain that this mistake has caused you."

The word "mistake" hit Heyer like an electric shock.

"It was a thread that ran through everything that had happened in my life," he says. "It was a mistake what grandma did. It was a mistake what my uncle did. It was a mistake to believe Walker. It was a mistake to have the surgery. And it was a mistake that Walker admitted had happened. So here you have this thread that runs well over forty years that has the word mistake in it. My life had become a mistake."

The "mistake" was ongoing and relentless. Heyer was still struggling with his gender issues when, in 1991, his one-year contract with CityTeam ended. A friend told him of an opening in Southern California. The job as a chemical dependency technician would involve counseling drug and alcohol patients in a hospital's psychiatric ward, and it sounded promising. Even though he'd worked at CityTeam as Walt, he decided to apply for the new position as Laura Jensen—the name still on all his legal documents.

The fact that even he found that decision perplexing didn't stop him from doing so. And he got the job.

But even Heyer's closest friends were tiring of the situation, he recalls. He had moved away from the church that sustained him, and stopped writing his regular letters to the anonymous members there who'd been his safety net.

In Laura Jensen's new role, she was dealing with patients who were alcoholics and drug addicts with severe psychological disorders, including self-mutilation and schizophrenia. She took vital signs, led therapy sessions, and developed daily social events for the patients. She often worked with a staff psychiatrist whose work and approach with patients she admired, and within thirty days the doctor had asked if Jensen might be willing to meet with him in a clinical setting. They began meeting in his free time, and after three weeks he suggested that Jensen consult with some of his colleagues. He used a term with which she says she was unfamiliar, and which had never before been proposed as the root cause of her problems: dissociative disorder.

From a list of specialists, Laura Jensen chose a female psychiatrist who operated out of a posh office in Beverly Hills. The two began meeting, and their sessions continued for weeks until one day the doctor called her in and offered a diagnosis. She also offered a more common name for dissociative disorder: multiple personality disorder.

In order to survive her life's various traumas, including her parents' harsh discipline, her grandmother's dress-up play, and her molestation by an uncle, the psychiatrist explained that her psyche likely had fragmented into several pieces. Each personality was related to Walt Heyer, but each had a life and an agenda of its own. The doctor went on to conclude that Walt had opted for his surgery in Trinidad while under the influence of one of those alternate personalities. That's why he signed in as Andrea West, who inexplicably changed her name to Laura Jensen after the surgery. The operation was that personality's determined effort to eradicate Walt once and for all. The bad news: Having had the surgery, the doctor said, recovering Walt as her primary personality was going to be extremely difficult.

Unconvinced, Jensen sought and got a third opinion. It was the same. A fourth therapist, who specialized in treating patients with dissociative disorder, suggested Laura Jensen actually return to living full-time as Walt Heyer. The suggestion made enough sense to her that Laura Jensen, seeking a clean break, quit her job to become Walt Heyer again. An old friend at Toyota was kind enough to hire her through a temporary agency to work on a re- call campaign, and she was grateful for the opportunity to return to the car business, even in such a limited capacity.

She began working again as Walt. But she still spent her off hours as Laura.

The dual life strategy had failed once before, following the surgery in Trinidad. The difference this time was the sobriety that created in both personas an illusion of self-determination. The deal struck between Walt and Laura permitted quick changes of personality. It was an absurd existence in which name and gender were interchangeable, and ultimately didn't matter. This was now a survival game.

A therapist who specialized in dissociative disorder began using hypnosis during their sessions, and Heyer says she identified between thirteen and fifteen separate personalities inside the same body. After examining handwritten notes, journals, and documents, the therapist noted distinctive differences in penmanship depending on whether the material was written by Walt Heyer, Laura Jensen, or Andrea West. Andrea's signature was tight, small, and slanted left, for example. Laura's was bold and slanted right. Confronted with that evidence, Heyer says it was hard to deny the possibility that the consensus diagnosis of dissociative disorder could be accurate. Gender dysphoria might have been part of the problem, but its roots reached far, far deeper. And it helped explain why gender confirmation surgery had brought no relief. Could so many of Heyer's critical life choices been based on a misdiagnosis?

Laura Jensen, exhausted and looking for comfort, decided to leave Southern California and return to the Bay Area to be closer to her support team at the church in Foster City and the Thompson family who'd been so kind to her in the past. She rented a room from a woman who'd taken her in once before and began attending regular AA meetings. But when she tried to return to the church that had been the scene of her public transition back into the persona of Walt, she got some unexpected and devastating news.

She'd returned to church on a weekend, but that Monday pastor Jeff Farrar called. The church elders had met and decided it was not healthy for the congregation to see her still struggling, flipping back and forth between male and female. "I can't tell you not to come here, it's just a request," Jensen recalls Farrar telling her. "The elders would appreciate it if you wouldn't come to church here anymore."

Jensen understood their concerns and accepted the verdict. How was she going to handle isolation from the church to which she'd turned for support? But then, two weeks later, one of the church elders called. The other elders were in the room, and each took a turn on the phone offering an apology and inviting her back. The church is here to serve broken people, they said. You're still welcome here.

Advised by a new therapist that working a job would interfere with the intensive therapy required to treat her disorder, and living mostly as Laura Jensen, she spent the next year couch surfing, living in a donated camper, running errands for a restaurant in exchange for meals, and waiting for a verdict on the application that would decide whether or not she qualified for permanent disability income. Approval would mean the chance to devote herself fully to therapy and recovery.

The fourth step of a twelve-step recovery program involves writing out a searching and fearless moral inventory of oneself. It's an exercise in identifying resentments, pain, and unresolved issues before turning all of that over to a higher power of choice. Asked by a Christian therapist to do so, Laura Jensen began to write. And write. For most people, the inventory is contained on a few pages. Laura wrote more than a hundred. After a session lasting several hours, she and the therapist retreated to the parking lot and burned the pages to—at least symbolically—turn all that pain and resentment into ash.

Back inside the office, Laura prayed with the therapist. She doesn't remember specifically what they prayed about, but says what happened next was unforgettable. She experienced the kind of personal vision of Jesus Christ sometimes described by born-again Christians. Jesus was dressed all in white, she recalls, with his feet hidden under his robe. He approached and took her into his arms, saying, "You are now safe with me forever."

Jensen began to cry. Looking back, she says she knew then and there that she would someday, somehow recover. "That was the point of redemption and restoration that changed everything."

As was so often the case in her life, that turning point was gradual and difficult. But she felt an important truth had been revealed. Walt Heyer/Laura Jensen wasn't a woman trapped in a surgically altered man's body, or a man trapped inside that resculpted female body. That person was an alcoholic with dissociative disorder.

Finally, some certainty.

With Jesus on her side, and the letter from Paul Walker apologizing for the "mistake" of his treatment and diagnosis, the messy bundle of complications and contradictions that began life as Walt Heyer felt prepared to move forward. Still, the rollercoaster ride would last for another five years.

18

Claudine Meets Karen

In October 2000, Claudine Griggs was hiking with a lesbian group called Southern California Women for Understanding in Orange County's Crystal Cove State Park when she met a fellow hiker named Karen Paley.

Paley, an assistant professor of English at Loyola Marymount University in Los Angeles at the time, was a recent transplant to Long Beach from relatively homogenous New England, and, for the first time in her life, she was a minority in a group she had joined. Long Beach has a strong and active gay community, and also is a melting pot of cultures from all over the world with nearly fourteen percent of its residents being African American and nearly as many Asians. Its Cambodia Town section, also known as Little Cambodia, is one of the largest Cambodian settlements outside of that country. Adding to Paley's discomfort was her unusual career status as a Jew teaching at a Jesuit university.

"Although I had been in a previous relationship with another woman, I had never had a period of really coming out into the gay community," Paley recalls. "I had not been out all that long myself, having come out of a twenty-nine-year marriage to a man, only to head into a five-year relationship with a woman who kept on with her ex throughout. I was still adjusting to the mix of peoples."

She and Griggs hit it off that day, and again at the group's Christmas dance two months later. She still had no idea Griggs was a transgender woman, but the topic had been on her mind. The previous spring she had conducted an exercise with her Western Lit students. She had asked the students to write down some of their prejudices on a board in the classroom. They'd been reading Amy Tan's *The Joy Luck Club*, and she remembers one of the prejudices listed on the board was "Asians can't drive."

The other prejudice she remembers clearly was one she had written on the board herself: transsexuals. Paley considered herself a fair and open-minded person, but she conceded that she had a tough time understanding that particular subset of humanity. "I knew two women in some support groups who were trans," Paley recalls, "and looking back, it was just personality stuff that annoyed me. I generalized that to a trans prejudice."

About a month after she met Griggs, Paley settled down with her Sunday *Los Angeles Times*, and the topic of transgenderism was staring her in the face.

The cover story of the *Los Angeles Times Magazine* that week, by *Times* staff writer and Pulitzer Prize winner Michael Hiltzik, was a gripping yarn about a supercomputer project at IBM in the late 1960s. It was called "Project Y," and a young researcher delving into the history of the project had run into a baffling dead end. IBM had lost nearly all records of the work, "as if having experienced a corporate lobotomy," Hiltzik wrote. Published details were scant, and the researcher was having trouble finding anyone who knew much about it.

A few days after posting a query about it on the Internet, the researcher received an email from a woman named Lynn Conway, a preeminent computer scientist, who seemed to know pretty much everything about the secret project. She had many of its records, too. Her knowledge level was jarring. How many women could have been involved in an IBM supercomputer project in the 1960s? And why did her name not appear anywhere among the team members who worked on it? How did she know?

Thus began Hiltzik's story, titled "Through the Gender Labyrinth," which revealed Conway's little-known past as one of the country's transsexual pioneers. She'd worked on the project under her male birth name.

"Nature directs living things into a vast maze of sexual diversity from which our culture provides only two acceptable exits: male and female," Hiltzik wrote in that story. "Gender is the most fundamental component of our self-image, the foundation of the personality we present to everyone around us. Think of the very first question one asks about a newborn: 'Is it a boy or a girl?'"

Hiltzik recounted how the intricacies of gender had worked their way into cultural, scientific, and even political debates of the time, sparking conversations about everything from lagging math scores among girls, to rough-play encouragement among boys, to the precise calculus of gender identity. He quoted George Brown, a psychiatrist at the Veterans Administration Medical Center in Johnson City, Tennessee, saying: "There's a little bit of each gender in each person, so there's something intriguing about what exists on the other side."

But Hiltzik also noted a certain cultural wariness about exploring a subject such as transsexualism, which he described as "the most extreme expression of gender discordance" and one of our culture's last taboos. "So strong is the stigma, so blatant the discrimination, that most keep the change a secret by shedding their old lives, jobs, and friends along with their old gender. Lynn Conway, among the first Americans to undergo a sex change, came to give the secret life into which it forced her a name: 'stealth.'"

Paley's new friendship with Griggs was quickly evolving into something more, but she still had no idea that their friendship would become part of that highly charged conversation. When Paley visited Griggs at her home just before Christmas, Griggs handed her a gift to commemorate the holiday. Inside were copies of two nonfiction books that Griggs had written about transsexualism, including her 1995 *Passage Through Trinidad* and a 1998 book called *S/He: Changing Sex and Changing Clothes*, which focused on the attitudes of transgender people about dress, body, and culture.

"They were wrapped and I told her not to open them until she got home," Griggs says. "I couldn't bear the thought of instant rejection by opening the gift there, but I wanted her to have the information quickly so that if rejection happened, I could get it over with before I fell too hard in love. This was always a problem for me in dating. Meet someone, start to care, tell them I was transsexual, and receive something like, 'You're a nice girl, but...' The rest was irrelevant. It always meant the same thing. No transsexuals allowed."

Paley says she realized when she opened Griggs's gift at home that her new friend was sending her a message. She called immediately and blurted her suspicion: "Are you a transsexual?"

"Yes," Griggs conceded.

Paley was stunned. The two trans women she'd met at that point in her life had made her uncomfortable. One was still recovering from gender confirmation surgery and, dressed like a woman from the 1950s, seemed far too fragile to be up and around. The other was loud, impulsive, and struggling with addiction issues that occasionally sent her back into a life of crime.

Now someone that Paley liked a lot was telling her she was trans?

Paley spent a week reading Griggs's books and discussing the situation with friends. At one point, one of them, whom Paley had previously held in high regard, posed a startling question: "Would you really want to be intimate with someone like that?"

Paley startled herself with her answer: "Well yes, I would."

19

Transition in Trinidad

Stanley Biber had always seemed tireless, just as he had been back in Korea when he powered through thirty-seven consecutive surgeries before passing out. By the late 1990s, he was still maintaining the busy schedule of a small-town surgeon. He continued to balance about three gender confirmation surgeries a week with his other medical duties, and still was running a massive cattle ranch, even participating in cattle drives. And he continued to hit the gym, occasionally rolling up his sleeves to show off his impressive biceps. But truth be told, time was gaining on him.

By September 2003, at age eighty, he told the *Pueblo Chieftain* newspaper that he hadn't operated on anyone in nearly three months and was turning down gender confirmation surgery patients from all over the globe. He'd been paying about $40,000 a year for malpractice insurance, but his long-time carrier had moved out of state, and at his age he'd been unable to convince another insurer to take him on at a rate he could afford. He was considered high risk, a designation generally applied to doctors older than sixty-five, and while one insurer seemed willing to cover him for about twice that amount for a short time, the high-risk status eventually would put his premiums at between $200,000 and $300,000 a year.

In addition, Biber's reputation was starting to wobble a bit as he aged. "Generally, he had a good rep," says transgender historian Susan Stryker, who was not a Biber surgical patient but who has many trans friends who were. "Solid. Affordable. Get you in and get you out. No fuss no muss. Not a big production number."

But grumbling had begun even as Biber helped train a new generation of surgeons in his techniques. In 1998, Dr. Gordene MacKenzie, a University of New Mexico professor of transgender theory and author of *Gender Nation*, told a writer for Denver's *Westword* magazine that she was no longer recommending Biber as a surgeon, an opinion echoed in that story by another source who said, "His age is starting to show."

When Biber began specializing in gender confirmation surgery, he had little competition. In the early days, after big university clinics either shut down or lost interest in gender research, Biber stood out among for-profit providers because of his reputation for surgical skill and compassion. Word spread fast in the worldwide transgender community. Other surgeons not only learned his techniques, but sometimes improved on them. Nancy Nangeroni, executive director of the International Foundation for Gender Education in Waltham, Massachusetts, told *Westword* in 1998 that she would not choose Biber personally because "it's too much of a cookie-cutter approach."

Biber, sensing his surgical career was nearing its end, wasn't shy about sharing his frustration. "I guess they think I'm too old," he told *Chieftain* reporter Mike Garrett, adding that no insurer would ever say that for fear of being sued for age discrimination. "I'm in tremendous physical condition, the best physical condition you can imagine. I work out every day and I've had no physical problems. I've very rarely been sued over the years and never by any of my transsexual patients. I'm still hoping I can pick up some insurance so I can continue working."

He was still able to see general practice patients at his downscale office above Trinidad's First National Bank. But surgery? Despite his half century of experience, that was out of the question without insurance.

Mary Lee Biber, the surgeon's widow, says Biber's transition from swaggering, world-renowned surgeon back to being a simple general practitioner was extremely difficult for him. But clearly Biber had seen that day coming. He'd already been auditioning other surgeons, inviting them to Trinidad to observe his techniques, gauging their interest, evaluating their suitability. One of them, from Seattle, seemed well prepared for the role.

Her name was Marci Bowers.

Mark Bowers was a standout student at the University of Wisconsin in Madison, graduating in 1980 with a bachelor's degree in medical microbiology. He then attended the University of Minnesota Medical School in Minneapolis, receiving his medical degree in 1986. While doing a four-year residency in obstetrics and gynecology at the University of Washington in Seattle, he married wife Ann and they had three children while embarking on what, by all accounts, was a comfortable doctor-track life. As his reputation grew, he eventually rose to the post of department chair at Seattle's respected Swedish Medical Center, along the way delivering more than 2,200 babies while there.

By the winter of 1996, though, the decision he'd been considering for years was no longer avoidable. He'd managed to shove it to the back of his mind during his most intense years of college and med school, even as he created a family and established himself as a professional. What was missing, though, was a sense of personal satisfaction with who he was. He was certain that he was a woman.

And so began a transition process that culminated with surgery in 1998. Dr. Mark Bowers became Dr. Marci Bowers. And post-op Marci Bowers was happy. What she once said of her transgender patients could also be said of her, "Transitioning is like walking on lily pads: You have to be careful with each step, or you're going to sink. It takes a lot of money, courage, and a certain amount of planning."

But she liked what she saw in the mirror every day. "I don't mean that in a narcissistic way. It was just the satisfaction that, 'Dang, I really look good and I look like me.' It's not just about looks, it's the person you become, the person you always felt yourself to be. There's a deep satisfaction to that. And you don't believe it for the first year or two. Gender is a social construct. It's not genitals, it's not even hormones, it's all these other little bells and whistles you do to announce your identity."

Besides, she says, to deny her true gender would have been like trying to stop something unstoppable. Bowers takes the long view, seeing gender in terms of human evolution. She uses the concept of entropy—in a broad sense, meaning the degree of disorder or uncertainty in a system—to explain. Humans are biological beings, and biology—as one small aspect of evolution—is part of a relentless process of becoming. Trying to control that relentless evolutionary march is like trying to control a mighty river. You can do so for a while, even a long while, but without intervention that river will just go back to becoming whatever it wants to become.

"The Missouri is the longest river in the United States, and it's the most realigned river in history," Bowers says of the 2,300-mile waterway. "Man has done all sorts of things to move the river, to divert it, to shove it a different direction for our own purposes. Well, guess what? There's so many people suing the Army Corps of Engineers because they've successfully moved the rivers—but the river doesn't want to be there. They've created all these floodplains and people have been pushed out of their homes and lives destroyed because the river used to go where it wanted to go, and now it's forced to go a different direction."

That's the thing people who don't understand transgenderism often overlook, Bowers says. You can impose a binary view of gender on the world if you wish. Male. Female. Little in between. But that's not in any way how nature works. Nature doesn't want order. Nature wants diversity. That eventually takes hold, and nature controls destiny. Even many people within the trans community subscribe to the gender-binary view of the world, wishing to become clearly one gender or the other, when—if entropy has its way—there's a lot of territory in the middle.

"It's complicated, because there are so many people that want to push people back into that little box," Bowers says of the binary view of gender, which is a big part of what makes transitioning so difficult in many modern cultures. "You have to be strong. This is not for the faint of heart."

When telling their stories, many trans men and women offer accounts no less nuanced and complicated than the stories of Griggs, Heyer, and Bowers. Facing a simplistic question such as

"Did surgery improve your life?" their answers almost always have a "Yes, but..." quality. Historian Susan Stryker says that's usually where it ends up for most post-op patients.

"I always try to keep in mind that surgery is a violent practice, a subtractive practice more often than not," Stryker says. "It doesn't make new tissue, it just takes what's there and rearranges it. Nerves get cut. It's a hard thing to happen to your body even if you really want it and even if it's better, even if it's, 'I've never felt attached to that thing that was attached to me, and I'm so much happier with that slippery little mango down there! That suits me. That's what I want.' And yet there can be so many problems with dilation, or there's problems with fistulas. It's hard to keep the opening open, or it's dry, it's imperfect. People don't make bodies as well as nature makes bodies.

"And yet, what most trans people I know get around to thinking and feeling is that 'I'm not holding myself to the standard that the only good body is a cis[gender] body. I feel this incredible sense of ownership of my body, I feel autonomy over it. I feel like I made a really significant decision about what I wanted to support my sense of self and communicate that to other people. Yes, I know there are problems. And it's better.' So if your standard of success is not 'How flawlessly cisgender passing is this?' but 'Does it satisfy my needs and accomplish my goals? And can I live in this body?'—the answer is yes.

"I know so many people who go down their mental checklist, 'If it turns out like this, would I be OK with it? If it turns out like that, would I be OK with that? Is there something that could happen that I really couldn't live with?' So I think people are very aware. They're not looking at it with rose-colored glasses."

Bowers is more blunt. "What's amazing is that the suicide rate is not actually higher after transition because there are just so many negatives for people who do it. It's a hard, hard thing to go through. But you can't alter the river. The river's gonna run through it."

Bowers wasn't naive enough to assume her battle would be over after she transitioned and had her surgery in 1998. But she concedes she wasn't fully prepared for the fallout that followed.

She'd managed to shut out the voices of friends and colleagues who warned her there'd be a professional price to pay for transitioning into life as a woman. Her practice did slow for a while, she says, but within two years she had as much business as ever. She was still a star at Swedish Medical Center, one of the largest hospitals in Washington state. She also was working at the Polyclinic, a respected multi-specialty clinic in downtown Seattle. But things started to sour during her transition.

"What I didn't know was how quickly you can fall from grace," she recalls. "At that time, [transitioning] just wasn't the 'in' thing. It was mostly lists of horrors. Certainly there were people who got it already, but people divided up very quickly and the problem is that there were just enough of the fearful and hateful people. So there were people against me and I didn't really realize how that worked."

Her employers seemed less comfortable with Marci Bowers than they had been with Mark Bowers, a situation similar to experiences described by many transgender people who experience a familiar set of post-op problems. Job descriptions change, transfers are arranged, positions are suddenly eliminated. "The bottom line is they eventually made me an offer I couldn't refuse," Bowers says, "which is what happens to so many trans folks. It's not from [the transition], it's always something else. That happened to me. I was shocked. I took my patients with me to private practice, but private practice was not easy. So I began looking at other jobs."

She was operating in "stealth" mode—the term Lynn Conway and many other transgender men and women use to describe their efforts to simply pass in life as a transitioned male or female—when she interviewed for the position of medical director for Planned Parenthood of Western Washington. "I wasn't really out, because I was really planning to go deep underground and not tell my story, which was how it used to be," she says. But she believes someone at the organization learned about her transgender status, and what seemed like a promising job prospect suddenly wasn't. The same thing happened when she interviewed for a position with another Seattle-area medical group operated by a conservative religious group.

"We got to the point where these guys were measuring the drapes for my office, then a drug rep came in and outed me," she claims. "'Adding a new partner? Dr. Bowers? Do you know all about Dr. Bowers?'"

One day a colleague, Marsha Botzer, suggested that Bowers meet Stanley Biber. Botzer is a foundational figure in the Seattle LGBTQ community, having started the now internationally known Ingersoll Gender Center in 1977 to provide support services for those struggling with gender issues. In the center's early years, Botzer, who understood firsthand the isolation and hunger for information among transgender men and women, had spread the word about the center by pulling the few books about gender issues from the area's library shelves and hiding business cards bearing the center's contact information inside their pages.

"There was no Internet back then, no way to reach out," she recalls. "So that's how people would find us."

Over the decades, Botzer says she made more than a hundred trips to Trinidad, often accompanying patients she'd met through the center as they journeyed to the remote Colorado outpost for surgery. During those years she became close to Biber, so close that eventually Biber gave her access to the records of his transgender patients. She used that information, anonymously, to survey those patients about their satisfaction level with their surgery and their post-op lives.

"It took several years to get to know him by just showing up," Botzer says. "Over those years we got to respect each other professionally, and that opened the possibility for a kind of friendship. I deeply appreciated his good work. I saw his skill and passion in the operating room. He was superb."

Bowers was not the first surgeon Botzer accompanied to Trinidad. She knew Biber was getting older, and that someone eventually would need to carry on his practice. He'd once told her that the day he could no longer trust his hands was the day he'd stop doing surgery, and she says she knew that someday "time and circumstance" would diminish his skills. But while she'd urged and even accompanied other doctors to visit Biber and watch him work, she says Bowers was "the first one to take it all the way."

Bowers had heard Biber's name, but knew little about the Trinidad surgeon. By then, Biber no longer was the only prominent name in the business. Dr. Eugene Schrang was doing more than a hundred gender confirmation surgeries a year at the Theda Clark Medical Center in Neenah, Wisconsin, a community of about 23,000 people. And Bowers's own surgeon, Dr. Toby Meltzer, was operating successfully out of Scottsdale, Arizona.

Besides, Bowers and had never seriously considered specializing in the kind of surgery she'd had herself. But on May 25, 2000, she traveled to Trinidad to meet the man her colleague had described as "a legend," and to watch him perform one of his trademark genital surgeries.

Biber was seventy-seven years old at the time and was wrestling with the idea of legacy. Thousands of his former patients, some calling themselves the "Biber Girls," were living apparently happier lives. He'd inadvertently put Trinidad on the map, at least in terms of the worldwide transgender community. But as he looked around the country, it was hard to imagine any other specialists who might relocate to his remote outpost in southern Colorado to apprentice with him and carry on his work.

"No one was coming up," Bowers recalls. "Eugene Schrang was a good surgeon, but he was in his seventies. Toby Meltzer was my age, but he refused to train anybody. He felt the pie was small and finite and would never grow. That was his fear. So he didn't want to divide his share of the pie. He knew he had a good gig going and he didn't want to give it up or expand it. There were a couple of other minor players, but there basically wasn't anybody doing it—and certainly nobody with my background or insight or history. It was just a field waiting to be tapped."

Even though Biber mentioned the idea of mentoring her during their visit and offered to teach her his techniques,

Bowers wasn't really considering the idea of relocating to Trinidad. "He said you should bring your husband down. I didn't have a husband at the time, but…"

About a year later, shortly after the terror attacks of September 11, 2001, Bowers traveled to Galveston, Texas, to attend for her first time a meeting of WPATH, the nonprofit professional association for transgender health. At the time, it was still called the Harry Benjamin International Gender Dysphoria Association, and in those days the conference was much smaller than it eventually would become. There she found herself socializing in a hotel pool with Biber and Pierre Brassard, whose Montreal clinic was the leading center for gender confirmation surgery in Canada. Both men were wearing Speedos, Bowers recalls, and they spent their time together talking about other specialists and centers of gender confirmation surgery.

She didn't realize it at the time, but the conversation would end up changing the trajectory of her life. "Those two ultimately became my mentors," she says. "They planted the seed."

———————

It's hard to say exactly how the courtship between Stanley Biber and Marci Bowers unfolded. Biber had invited many surgeons to Trinidad to learn from him, always with an eye toward finding the one who might someday take on his practice. Bowers likes to tell a version that includes intriguing hints of destiny along the way, including a moment when Biber handed her his scalpel in the middle of a surgery—a metaphorical passing of the torch—and a double rainbow that arced over Mt. San Rafael Hospital the night before that happened. "It's things like that that tell me it's more than an accident that I'm here," Bowers once told a reporter. She also described Biber as her "spiritual father," and more recently explained Biber's decision to choose her this way:

"Some didn't have the hands. Some didn't have the courage. Some didn't have the heart. When I finally came, he said Marci is the only one to have all three."

No matter how it happened, in January 2003, nearly three years after paying her first visit to meet Biber, Bowers was ready to take a chance. Although still married to her wife, the mother of their three children, Bowers was living apart from her family and was dating a transgender man, a specialist in deep-tissue Reiki massage. With her boyfriend and her youngest son, who was about seven at the time, Bowers packed up her life in Seattle and moved to Trinidad to train with Biber and eventually take over the dual role of surgeon and gender confirmation surgery specialist that Biber had played since 1969.

There was a certain comfort to her new life in Trinidad, a town that during Biber's decades as a specialist had grown accustomed, if not entirely comfortable, with the transgender pilgrims who frequented its hotels, restaurants, clothing shops, and other businesses. Their presence in town was still a source of occasional conversation, but the place was generally welcoming and the locals appreciated the business. Bowers settled in and began training with Biber to carry on his work.

The more surgeries she did, the more she refined Biber's time-tested techniques. He was by all accounts an old-school surgeon, even reluctant to employ a laparoscope long after that less invasive surgical technique became the standard for gallbladder and other surgeries. It was the same with genital surgeries. With a few modifications, he'd pretty much been using the same techniques pioneered by French surgeon Georges Borou, which Biber had learned from those early drawings he cadged from Dr. John Hoopes at Johns Hopkins in 1969.

Bowers, though, was seeing the possibility of some innovations, particularly in terms of improving the post-op genital sensitivity in her patients. In the genetic soup from which all humans develop, the clitoris is sort of a miniature version of the penis—a homolog, in biological terms, meaning a biological structure with a shared ancestry such as the forelimbs of vertebrates. (For example, bat wings, human arms, and whale flippers are all roughly the same basic structure, or homologous.) Both the clitoris and the penis have a similar set of nerve endings that make them particularly sensitive during sex.

Biber's technique didn't leave his patients with what Bowers calls a "true homologous clitoris," but she saw ways to use the available erectile tissues to improve sexual sensitivity in those for whom she was creating a vagina. "You don't necessarily need a clitoris to orgasm, or have a penis," she says. "We know this from trauma victims. If the penis is amputated, you can still orgasm."

In the beginning, she copied Biber's surgical techniques exactly as he showed her. Then she began refining, knowing it would be a process of trial and error, but certain that she could improve the results. She also wanted to cut surgical times, always a plus when anesthesia is involved. But even as she refined, she says she understood Biber's reasons for sticking with the techniques he'd spent decades perfecting.

"Many surgeons reach a certain point in the refinement of what they do where they're comfortable and they're busy and they have people coming in the door, patients don't have complications, and that's it," Bowers says. "That's as far as they evolve. That does two things. First, it offers consistency for patients. They know what they're getting. But second, it leaves the door open for somebody to do something better. I think he knew he didn't necessarily have the most refined techniques, but I think he was holding the door for me to come in and to go further."

If Bowers had simply stepped through that door and quietly assumed Biber's role as Trinidad's most famous surgeon, the professional transition might have gone smoothly. And for a few years, it did. Bowers is friendly and likable, and easily made friends in town. She enjoyed playing the local golf courses. The relationship with her boyfriend ultimately faltered, but she met and began dating a gregarious local woman named Carol Cometto, who at the time was the director of golf at Trinidad's municipal course.

Cometto had been delivered by Stanley Biber at Mt. San Rafael Hospital, and had spent a lot of time at Biber's home following the early death of her mother. "I ate at Doc's house more than I ate at my own," she remembers. For nineteen years she played with "Doc's Patients," the softball team that Biber sponsored and coached, and recalls one game where a tough slide play at third base left her with broken ribs. Biber ordered her into the dugout, told her to take off her shirt, and move the elastic bandage from her knee and wrap it tightly around her ribs. Then he sent her back into the game. Afterward, Biber audaciously sent Cometto's Italian-immigrant father a bill.

"My dad marched up to his office and said, 'I no pay,'" Cometto recalls. And Biber, chastened, tore up the bill on the spot.

Cometto, a dog lover and out-and-proud lesbian, is among the most visible people in Trinidad, working at Tire Shop Liquors, a high-end downtown liquor and wine store, and tooling around town in a truck with hand-painted, multi-colored paw prints all over it. During a driving tour of the city, she recalled a love-at-first-sight scenario when she met Bowers. At the time, she had no idea the attractive new woman in town was a doctor, much less a renowned surgeon. "I didn't even know she was a changer!" Cometto recalls, using a term she and her friends often used to describe Biber's transgender patients. Until a friend clued her in, she had no idea that Dr. Marci Bowers used to be Dr. Mark Bowers.

One day in 2006, she says she was on the golf course when a coworker tracked her down. She'd had an urgent call from Biber, asking her to come to the surgeon's office right away. She balked, but the look in her coworker's eyes made clear this was no ordinary situation. At Biber's downtown office, she joked about how the surgeon made her wait all the time when she came for an appointment, and wondered why he couldn't wait for her to finish her round of golf. But Biber wasn't in a joking mood. He'd heard a rumor that Marci Bowers was considering leaving Trinidad because her boyfriend had left town.

Cometto and Bowers were getting romantically involved, and Cometto also was an important social bridge between Biber and Trinidad's sometime skeptical locals who always had been comfortable with Biber, if not his patients. "He said, "Kid, you gotta do everything in your power to keep her here,'"

Cometto recalls. "I said I would, and I tried my hardest. He didn't want just anybody to take it over. But he definitely wanted his legacy to live on."

Until that point, things had seemed promising. Just a year after taking over Biber's practice, Bowers was doing about three gender confirmation surgeries a week— about the same number as during Biber's prime. But it also was becoming clear that Marci Bowers was not content to simply step into Biber's role. She intended to intensify the spotlight on Trinidad—and on her own unusual story.

20

Trouble in Trinidad

Stanley Biber, who often drove an ancient, battered Toyota pick-up and who for decades worked out of a musty office building with all the charm of a nineteenth-century sanitorium, offered the same basic piece of advice to a lot of different people in his life: If you've got it, don't flaunt it.

He dressed like the rancher he was, including Western shirts, cowboy boots, and what appears in photos to have been a manly black Stetson. He'd put on a suit if he had to, but reserved that chore mostly for medical conferences and speaking engagements staged far from Trinidad where he often was a featured speaker. His house was virtually indistinguishable from the nondescript cattle-country houses that dot the landscape around Trinidad. Biber spent his money to buy land, and even though he eventually amassed more of it than just about anyone else in Las Animas County, Colorado, not many people seemed to know that.

"He'd buy land, but no nice cars, no nice houses," recalls longtime financial advisor Kelly Tucker. "He had a farm house, a house in town, a ranch house. But none of these were nice. He called no attention to himself as far as money. He didn't dress well. You couldn't pick him off the street as having a nickel."

When it came time to talk about what he did for a living, Biber was no shrinking violet. He had a surgeon's ego, and willingly cooperated with reporters from regional and national publications who sought him out for interviews and profiles. His story was told by Oprah Winfrey, Geraldo Rivera, and countless others who shined their bright lights in Biber's direction. But he apparently did not employ a publicist, and while he made himself available to those who wanted to tell his story, he didn't actively seek media coverage. He saw publicity opportunities as chances to educate the public about transgender men and women and the compassion they deserved.

"He was a very humble man," says Kim Lucero, a Trinidad native who occasionally saw Biber as a patient, and who became a marketing and media spokesperson for Mt. San Rafael Hospital after Biber handed off the surgical duties to Bowers. "He just wanted to help people. He didn't want notoriety or recognition for it. He wasn't shy about publicity, but he didn't flaunt it or over-publicize it either."

Biber's handpicked protege took a different approach, in a number of ways. In contrast to Biber, who dedicated his entire medical career to Trinidad and its residents and the transgender pilgrims who sought him out, Bowers came to town as an outsider. She kept an office in Seattle, where her wife and children lived, and continued to treat obstetrical patients there after moving to Trinidad via a nurse practitioner and, later, a fellow obstetrician. "It was an odd delusion for me—I never imagined I'd actually remain in Trinidad."

When she was in Trinidad, for at least the final months of her time there, Bowers tooled around in a used Porsche Boxster. It's not that those things didn't sit well with the locals; Bowers was by most accounts liked and respected by both patients and the citizenry. But her relatively flashy personal style highlighted the differences between herself and her beloved predecessor, with whom nearly everyone had some personal and affectionate acquaintance.

"She didn't have the same persona that Dr. Biber had," recalls Alfred "Bucky" Carr, who worked as the nurse anesthetist for Biber from the early 1990s until 2002, before leaving for another job near Boulder, Colorado. And while his time with Bowers was limited during the period when Biber was helping mentor his replacement, Carr did have enough exposure to Bowers to compare and contrast the two. "She was more aloof, where Dr. Biber warmed right up to anybody that met him."

The big rub, though, apparently involved publicity. Like Biber, Bowers saw media exposure as a useful tool in educating the public about transgender issues. She saw herself as playing an important role in "educating and informing the nation and the world about the lives and characters of those who seek transgender surgery and about being trans." But Lucero recalls the tensions that arose as Bowers invited reporters and film crews to document her work. Print reporters and photographers were less intrusive than the TV and film teams that brought cameras, microphones, and general chaos to the twenty-five-bed hospital. But both print and broadcast media began arriving in a steady flow not long after Bowers took the reins from Biber. Eventually the hospital board decided to institute a policy requiring a sixty-day advance notice to the hospital before such visits, and also wanted to charge media outlets for access.

"Media could come and go, and they were in and out of here like crazy" during the Bowers years, Lucero recalls. "That's no way to run a community hospital. When you have HIPAA (the federal legislation that protects patient privacy and medical information) and all these other things you have to uphold, there are some rules and guidelines that I was very sticky about. When cameras were rolling, we needed consent forms."

Film crews also occasionally wanted to get out of the hospital and shoot footage of Bowers during her off hours. Since she likes to play golf, it was logical to accompany her to one of the local courses. It's one thing to play in or behind a foursome that includes a transgender woman. Trinidad was by then accustomed to such scenes. But a film crew on the course? That was another issue altogether.

"They were building a Jack Nicklaus-designed golf course out east of town," says Cometto, who by then had become Bowers's lover, referring to the now-mothballed Cougar Canyon development, which opened in 2008 about the time the US economy began a long, painful nosedive. "It was a fabulous golf course, and they were building all these nice homes around there. Big plans. Nah nah nah nah."

One of its primary developers was a powerful man in town who not only was involved in the local golf association, but also was on the board at Mt. San Rafael Hospital. "Well, this guy didn't want the retirement community to be mingled up with the transgenders, and he made it rough for Marci," Cometto says. "When the film crews would come, we'd go play golf. And if there were other transgender people before their surgeries, they'd want to take them out to play golf, too. And the golf association hated that. They actually had the churches go against her. The hospital board. They went against her and made it rough for her."

Cometto's version is a bit oversimplified, but basically accurate. In truth, Mt. San Rafael was going through a transition of its own. For decades it had offered Biber's transgender patients significant discounts on their surgical work because that work generally was not covered by insurance. It continued to do so after Bowers took over. But at a time when community hospitals were struggling to make their finances work, the hospital board began taking a hard look at whether or not it could continue to do so. Ultimately it chose to reduce those discounts, increasing the out-of-pocket expenses for Bowers's patients.

Things came to a head in 2007. Trinidad was finding itself more in the public spotlight than ever. According to a 2007 feature story in *The Denver Post*, the BBC came to town to produce a six-part series on Bowers and her adopted hometown. She was on *The Tyra Banks Show* and did a guest gig on the hit TV show *CSI*. CNN's *Paula Zahn Now* devoted a segment of its "Fighting for Acceptance" series to Bowers's work. During the middle of an interview with *Post* reporter Douglas J. Brown, Bowers took a call from her secretary. A television studio wanted Bowers to fly to Los Angeles to appear on a show.

"Yeah, right," Bowers replied with sarcasm. "That'll happen."

One critical point apparently came in 2007, during production of a short-lived reality television series called *Sex Change Hospital* that tracked a dozen transgender patients under Bowers's care at Mt. San Rafael. "Obviously something like that is labor-intensive, and it's stressful for our staff," Lucero says. "They want to take care of patients."

The hospital pushed back, Lucero says, and the increasingly tense relationship between the hospital and Marci Bowers began to fray.

21

Happy in Plain Sight

The diminutive woman leading the tour of Rhode Island College was keeping an assertive pace, opening doors for herself and putting one sneaker in front of the other so fast it was an effort to keep up as she moved across the campus of what in early spring 2018 was a 164-year-old institution. Her bobbed hair, no-nonsense eyeglasses, and maroon college sweatshirt marked her as a seasoned academic, but her dimples, toothy smile, and high energy could have belonged to a student one-third her age. During that cold early-spring day in New England, she was wearing a red parka with a hood fringed in dark faux fur. She was also wearing a blue baseball cap commemorating the Air Force Strategic Air Command at Vandenberg Air Force Base.

"Some of the students who were vets seem to prefer working with other vets," she explained. "Maybe it's time to quit hiding the fact that I'm a vet."

Claudine Griggs isn't hiding much of anything these days. During two days of interviews, she seemed to hold nothing back about her long-ago surgery in Trinidad, her decision to go public with her story despite the strong impulse to just fade quietly into the unremarkable life for which she longed, and the often difficult post-op road she had traveled to where she is today. The "Safe Zone" sign on her office door in the college's busy Writing Center, which she directs, draws a bright line for anyone who enters: "This space respects all aspects of people, including race, ethnicity, gender expression, sexual orientation, socioeconomic background, age, religion, and ability."

The story of how she got from Southern California to Rhode Island College offers an extended postscript for her remarkable journey. And it ultimately underscores the wisdom of her long-ago decision to detour her life through Trinidad.

Griggs and Karen Paley began a romantic relationship in 2000 for which Griggs had never dared hope, and Paley never imagined. But within a couple of years, as often happens with professional couples, Paley's career took an unexpected turn. In the summer of 2002, she got an offer for a tenure-track English professorship at Rhode Island College, about as far away from their lives in Southern California as was possible within the continental United States. But it was closer to Paley's hometown of Boston, where her father lived, and she decided to accept. Their story could have ended there.

But if Griggs understood anything after enduring decades of struggle and pain, it was that better days are not always beyond her grasp. She told Paley that if after a year she liked the Rhode Island College job and the city of Providence, then she'd be willing to take a chance, uproot her life, and move to be with her.

At the time, Griggs was working two part-time administrative jobs, one at an Irvine, California, law firm and the other as a writing center tutor and visiting professor of communications at Soka University in nearby Aliso Viejo. By then she had earned her BA and MA in English at California State Polytechnic University in Pomona, and had written two nonfiction books about transsexualism. She knew that leaving would be a leap of faith unlike any she had undertaken before, except perhaps her decision to first contact Stanley Biber. But in mid-2003, Griggs gave notice to her employers. She was heading east, away from the stable but ever-fragile life she had built for herself in the sunny southwest corner of the country.

In her *Journal*, Griggs had written of her occasional fantasy to move to a new city, a new state, and "start a life where I will never have to acknowledge (even to myself) that I am what I was." But the significance of the decision was far greater than a simple change of jobs or location. Besides, publishing her *Journal* had put an end to that fantasy. Her life by then was a public one, her past inescapable.

No, Griggs was actually allowing herself to dream again, daring herself toward the life she'd almost given up hope of living. "I wanted a family," she says. "Karen has strong connections to her sons, and grandchildren were coming. I took a chance on getting a new family since I had lost my biological family."

Of course, family implies a level of commitment, for better or worse. That reality struck within Paley's first few years back on the East Coast. Her grandkids arrived, but her father in Boston got sick. She needed to be involved in his care, and it was good that she was so close. Griggs continued writing, even trying her hand at her first love—science fiction—and eventually picked up some adjunct teaching positions at Rhode Island College and the University of Massachusetts at Dartmouth. During their early years in Providence, Griggs relied on her veteran's health-care benefits until she was eligible, after a year of residency, to be considered a domestic partner under Paley's full-time salary and benefits.

Like any other late-career couple massaging their benefit plans as they age, they built a mutual support safety net. In 2009, Paley developed a brain cyst that became increasingly debilitating as it grew. Her behavior became erratic and she was denied tenure, ending her full-time teaching career at Rhode Island College at the end of the 2008 academic year. She underwent brain surgery at Rhode Island Hospital in November 2009, but by then the couple's roles had begun to switch. In spring 2009, Griggs had interviewed for and was offered a position as director of the college's Writing Center. The job was considered part faculty and part college staff—one of the few positions on campus so defined—and it came with benefits, allowing Paley the freedom to change careers following her health scare. A lifelong hobby investor, she decided to turn pro. Paley became a financial advisor and, in 2017, took a job with Apple Federal Credit Union in Fairfax, Virginia, a position that led to relocation away from Rhode Island, and a two-year separation from Griggs.

Then, in April 2011, life dealt Griggs yet another unexpected hand. After a routine mammogram, she was diagnosed with Stage 1 metastatic cancer in her right breast. It had not yet spread to her lymph nodes, but the recommended treatment was a mastectomy. The treatment also required something that edged her into the realm of pure irony: Because her specific type of cancer was considered an estrogen receptor, she was immediately taken off the supplemental estrogen she had been taking for decades. After the mastectomy, her oncologist prescribed an estrogen blocker, reasoning that since her breasts had begun to develop when she was a teen even before she transitioned and began taking hormones, then her body was capable of producing some level of estrogen on its own. She would need to start taking estrogen blockers, which she says produced hot flashes that "contributed to global warming" and also caused joint pain and put her at risk for osteoporosis.

"That was a tough one," she says. "Part of me believed I'd rather die."

More than most, Griggs understood that it's impossible to make decisions about medical treatment without considering the individual involved. And she did have options, some of which might not have turned out well. "But I still had to consider the particular kind of cancer, and the treatment that followed—estrogen blockers—all of those things were part of what I had to deal with. When I was in the cancer group talking with people, many of whom had dismal prognoses, there were individualized treatments for each particular person, which seems to me to be the only way to deal with those kinds of issues. And I do consider transsexualism a medical issue because it requires treatment to help alleviate the issues involved, and the suffering."

She recalls a moment as she was being prepped for the mastectomy. She began to cry, to sob actually. When the nurses noticed her tears, she shut down the waterworks and assured the medical team that that would be the last time she cried about losing her breast.

"No," one of the nurses replied, "it's not."

Which turned out to be true. But Griggs endured the mastectomy and the follow-up treatments, and has been cancer-free since. After five years, she opted to discontinue the estrogen blockers, and even went back on estrogen supplements in early

2018 in her quest to feel "normal" again. She says she felt better almost immediately.

Along the way, other life complications continued to pop up like jack-in-the-box aggravations. For example, on August 1, 2013, Rhode Island became the tenth US state to allow same-sex marriage. Griggs and Paley decided to make their twelve-year partnership a legal union. They set their wedding date for August 16 and began the paperwork.

Things hit a snag when the time came to present their birth certificates. Decades earlier, Griggs had tried without success to force the state of Tennessee, where she was born, to change the gender designation on that document. At the time, Tennessee was the only state that did not allow that. To the city clerk, it made no difference that she was listed as Claudine Griggs, a female, on her US passport, driver's license, Social Security card, and veteran's ID. The clerk also dismissed the long-ago letter written and signed by Stanley Biber as "a doctor's note" that was simply irrelevant. She was listed as Claude Griggs on her birth certificate, and only a birth certificate could establish her identity, and that was that. No marriage license.

Griggs speaks for many transgender people when she talks about her longing for an uncomplicated life. Try to imagine the discomfort of standing publicly in a city office, haggling with the clerk and her deputies about your gender identity. The legal discussion, which eventually involved various attorneys, the mayor, and the Rhode Island Health Department, dragged on until the clerk eventually agreed to issue a marriage license in the name of "Claudine" only if Griggs agreed to legally change her name in Rhode Island. The city attorney arranged for an expedited probate court hearing, and they finally received an accurate marriage license two weeks after their wedding.

Rhode Island College senior Chelsea Riordan has worked for two years as a tutor in the college's Writing Center under Griggs's direction. She had no idea her boss was transgender until a fellow student read one of Griggs's books and filled her in. She was surprised, but mostly because she hadn't figured it out on her own. She says she's "really into queer theory" and involved in the LGBTQ community and a little baffled that Griggs's background caught her unawares. But learning the truth simply increased her respect for the woman she considers a bit of a mother hen to the struggling writers on campus.

"I naturally feel a kinship with someone when I find out they're not straight or cis," Riordan said. "It just makes them feel a little safer, like, 'Oh you get it. Cool.' But if you told me someone like her existed in a novel, it would seem a little too crazy. Her story is almost Forrest Gumpish in terms of history and how many things she's seen, and what she's managed to do in spite of where she comes from and all of the struggles that she's faced. She came out with a successful career, important books published, she's a professor, she's got a lovely wife, she's done so much and been so successful, I find her history very inspiring."

Riordan also said she's proud of Griggs, and immediately apologized for saying so. "Honestly, I feel weird saying that about someone who is many years older than me who is also my superior, because that's like something I would say to my cat, 'I'm so proud of you, bud.' But I am proud of her. I sort of struggle with the idiom 'What doesn't kill you makes you stronger,' but she has learned to use what hurt her in the past to make herself this strong. If she's this self-possessed, she's probably had it in her all along. But she's had such a wild life ... "

Just down the hall, Patrice Mettauer nodded her approval when talk turned to Claudine Griggs. Mettauer directs the college's office of student and academic support, of which the Writing Center is a part, and has worked with Griggs for three years. In her role overseeing the place where so many students come for help, Mettauer said she deals with a lot of young people who are struggling with social and gender issues. "So I watch these young people confronting this decision that Claudine confronted many years ago, it's ... "

She paused briefly to compose herself. "I don't know how they find the courage, I really don't. It's moving to me to watch them step out in a way that they know they're in danger with their peers, in danger walking the streets. To me, creating a safe environment where they know they're going to be OK is really important."

Mettauer said she didn't learn Griggs's full story until nearly a year into their work relationship, and for that period had no idea she was a transsexual woman. She has never known her as anything but a woman. But she did notice Griggs's unusually high level of anxiety about a year earlier as the college consolidated three different student support operations into a single facility. That meant relocating the Writing Center from the space it had occupied for many years into a larger shared space in the basement of the campus library.

To Griggs, she said, the move put at risk the welcoming, nonjudgmental culture of the Writing Center that she had nurtured during her time as its director. She'd helped create a space where students could express themselves freely—a freedom she'd wanted so desperately at an earlier point in her life. Would folding the center into a larger enterprise erode that culture? At the same time as the move, Griggs's longtime assistant, an instrumental part of creating and maintaining the Writing Center culture, retired. And on top of that, at about the same time, Mettauer asked Griggs to upgrade from a pen-on-paper scheduling system to an online system. It apparently made Griggs feel like something she cherished was slipping away.

"She may have been afraid that students wouldn't come anymore," Mettauer said, "that the Writing Center wouldn't be as successful in doing its work and in assisting students who needed the support. And in the first semester we did see a drop in the numbers. So I think that transition was really worrisome because of her commitment to what she does, to make people feel really good about writing. She's a Pied Piper in that way."

Later in the conversation, Mettauer circled back to that idea, still thinking about Griggs's passionate instinct to defend what she considers a safe space for self-expression. "I think about this idea of home," she says, "of home being our grounding when we're out adventuring in the world. We always come home. I think that's how Claudine felt about the Writing Center. It was home. And to have that foundation shaken up a bit was disconcerting to her."

Griggs's one-bedroom apartment near Rhode Island College is a bit of a writer's cave. She writes in the bedroom crowded with unpacked boxes from a June 2017 move, a desk, printer, computer, lamp, file cabinets, and a small sign that reads "writing center." She lives there alone, mostly, since Paley's job as a financial advisor is based in Fairfax, Virginia. Griggs visits her about once a month, and Paley heads north every couple of months. They look forward to the day when they no longer need to commute.

Griggs is clearly comfortable here. And her alone time gives her the chance to take long backward glances down the hard road she traveled. Despite her doubts, misgivings, and disappointments about the surgery she underwent at the hands of Trinidad's Stanley Biber, and despite her impatience with gender-rights activists who obsess about proper pronoun usage and their preferred vocabulary, she has arrived at a place of peace, and occasionally, even happiness. She knows enough to remain wary of that. But she also allows herself the pleasure of knowing, in the end, it all worked out pretty well.

In her *Journal*, Griggs ultimately justified her decision to undergo gender confirmation surgery with a quote from Tom Joad of John Steinbeck's *The Grapes of Wrath*: "It don't take no nerve to do somepin when there ain't nothin' else you can do."

But she focuses these days on the last part of that quote. Surgery isn't the only option for those suffering from gender dysphoria, she believes, and it's not the right choice for everyone. She understands at a profound level that surgery is a radical step, and she worries about those who approach that decision with misinformation, flawed assumptions, and anything less than abject despair. She thinks of surgery as the last, best resort for those who see the only other option as death.

"When I think about surgically or hormonally altering a body, I think of it as a very personal decision, and I think that person should have professional, informed advice regarding those decisions so that they don't do something that will harm themselves in the long run, or that they're not reacting to their own prejudices about what they think a man or woman should be, or what they think a liberated LGBT person should be," she says, sitting forward to emphasize her point. "When I start thinking about surgeries, or even hormone therapy, which is permanent after a very short time, they should be thinking about one individual at a time, not some blanket recommendation by any community, medical or otherwise."

In her case, she'd deeply resented the prescribed protocols to which she had to adhere when approaching her own surgery. Having lived for more than a decade as a woman before traveling to Trinidad, why did she need the medical community to ratify that? Why did she need statements from two mental health professionals to prove to Biber that she was psychologically suited for surgery? She considers that process of "jumping through hoops arbitrarily defined by different members of the medical community" as a bit of an insult, as do many others.

Marci Bowers, the surgeon who succeeded Biber in Trinidad, also resists the idea that someone seeking gender confirmation surgery needs the approval of mental health experts. That implies that the individual is ill-equipped to make the choice for themselves. "We have this layer [in the WPATH standards of care protocols] that a lot of activists disagree with, that we have to see a psychologist or psychiatrist because you're making this big change. It's pretty ridiculous that that is required."

Still, Bowers believes the standards, while imperfect, serve an important purpose. They force anyone seeking surgery to slow down and think about their decision, often for a long time. Insisting that they live as a member of their desired gender for at least a year before surgery is an important safeguard, because she often has patients who come to her with unrealistic expectations. Female-to-male patients tend to be fairly practical about the transition and surgery. "For them it's more 'I just want some validation about my maleness. I just want a penis, something I can stand up and pee with.'"

Male-to-female patients, on the other hand, sometimes "come still laden with this testosterone buzz, I guess you could say, where they think with a vagina they're gonna suddenly be the siren of the sea and draw people to them, that they'll be these equal sexual beings with other women. I think it's sometimes because they fantasize about the idea or imagine how wonderful it must be for women who are these magnets for sexual attention."

Either way, she says, these are incredibly complicated people trying to make a momentous life decision. Caution is wise.[25]

"I can tell you this: For me, if someone has been living as a woman or man for fifteen or twenty years, do you really think they're going to go back? Our current standard is one year. But do you think anyone who has lived for five years or more as a woman is ever going back?"

Griggs's experiences with unscrupulous or unqualified doctors and mental health professionals colors her thinking. But in hindsight, she says she appreciates the need for the WPATH protocols. "I like the idea of standards of care, and hopefully not just the medical community, but the patient would seriously consider those standards of care and why they exist. I think I did it in a good way for me, even though I didn't really want it that way. There were some bad doctors, and there were some bad policies. But I think it turned out well."

She sits back, reconsidering what she's just said. When she speaks again, she underscores the importance that the surgery played in her life. "I'm also saying that treatment can be life-saving. It can make the difference between a life that is impossible and a life that is possible. Surgery won't solve every problem. But for me it made life livable, and eventually life got pretty good, and eventually it was enjoyable—not every day, but whose life is?"

She's thrilled that a small independent publisher recently offered her a contract for her first novel, titled *Don't Ask, Don't Tell*, which she says revolves around a fictional underground organization that goes by that name. The group wants to avenge historic and contemporary injustices against gays and lesbians, and to obtain full legislated rights for that community. In the story, a San Francisco cop and a Pomona, California, detective suspect that two bizarre suicides are actually murders, and that the victims—a teetotaling Baptist preacher who died of a heroin overdose and a school board member who injected herself with cobra venom—are connected by their vitriolic homophobia. The suspicious officers—one a lesbian, the other Latino—launch an unofficial investigation and find more than expected.

Griggs later submitted her retirement notice to Rhode Island College, effective at the end of the following academic year. Since May 10, 2019, she has been enjoying life without the administrative work that goes along with an academic career. She has more time to write, she says in an upbeat email a few months after our in-person interviews, and she intends "to live happily ever after" with Karen Paley. As one might expect of someone who has never let optimism overwhelm her, Griggs adds a sardonic two-letter postscript:

"Ha!"

After everything she's endured—uncertainty, rejections, family alienation, violence, social indignities, physical pain, her difficult search for love and self-acceptance—the survival of her sense of humor is worth noting.

22

The Yo-Yo Years

Accepting Jesus Christ as a personal savior did not immediately simplify Walt Heyer's life. In fact, one might argue that between 1992 and 1996, it added yet another layer of complication. He was back on what he called "the yo-yo," alternating between living as Walt and then Laura, changing jobs each time he switched personas.

A friend who'd helped Heyer find a job at an oil company decided to start his own trucking company with a loan of $190,000 from another friend, and invited Heyer to become a partner. Maybe this was the fresh start he needed? But it was not to be. The plan crashed and burned, and in dramatic fashion. They were just weeks away from launching the gas-hauling business when Heyer's partner and his girlfriend decided to end their long-term relationship. And one day shortly after that, Heyer got a call from a mutual friend at his church. His new business partner had just put a plastic bag over his head and suffocated himself.

Heyer's response to that trauma? He became Laura Jensen again and got a job in a coffee shop.

The yo-yo continued to rise and fall, but the falls seemed to be particularly harrowing. His business partner's death was just one of a series of tragedies to befall critical friends and supporters during those years. Roy Thompson's disabled twenty-nine-year-old son, Jon, who had been struck by a car at age nine while standing on a sidewalk, and who waited for Laura at the bus stop each day while she was living with the Thompson family in Pleasanton, had contracted AIDS through a blood transfusion done years before, at a time when testing of the blood supply was sporadic rather than standard procedure. He finally succumbed, dealing another blow to Heyer's fragile equilibrium.

Heyer had always valued friendships, one of the few reassuring constants in his tumultuous life. That made the loss of those friends especially hard for him. One of his long-time counselors, Dr. Dennis Guernsey, was diagnosed with brain cancer and died not long after Heyer's final visit with him. Another close friend, Cathy, who'd taken in Heyer as Laura after he left a recovery program, was diagnosed with colon cancer. By the time it was discovered, the cancer already had spread to other organs. She was forty-six and terminal. Heyer became part of her support network as her health declined, along with one of Cathy's other friends. Her name was Kaycee.

The three of them occasionally shared a meal, and it quickly became clear that Cathy had told Kaycee the story about Heyer's gender and mental health struggles. Heyer was delighted that his past didn't seem to bother his new friend. "That was good for me, to have another person who knew and accepted my past, someone who was safe," he recalls.

A friendship began to blossom as Walt and Kaycee focused on helping their mutual friend during her illness. They began meeting alone for coffee, propping each other up during a sad and difficult struggle toward an impending loss. Heyer began to see Kaycee as something more than just a friend, but having undergone a deep spiritual experience, he began to view her arrival in his life as the work of a God in whom he believed wholeheartedly. But given his past and his still uncertain future, he was unable to fathom how such a relationship might unfold.

———

Heyer wasn't exactly a catch, romance-wise. In addition to his mental health issues and gender ambiguity, he was relying on permanent SSI disability to survive, and he lived in federally subsidized housing. While he doesn't consider himself a particularly political person ("My politics would be to take everybody in Washington and throw them all out on both sides," he says) he does tend toward the conservative side of things. He supported H. Ross Perot when he ran for president as an independent in 1992, for example, "not because he would have made a good president—he would have made a lousy president—but he would have stirred up Washington to the point where I would have enjoyed Washington." The idea of living off federal assistance bothered him, because he felt those twin realities should not be part of God's plan for his life.

After securing a Bay Area delivery job (as Walt) through a friend he'd known for years, he moved out of federal housing and, ten years after first moving in with the Thompson family, he moved back into their home. Besides, the move put him closer to his sick friend, Cathy, and her friend Kaycee.

About that time, he began to feel that living full-time as Walt Heyer was a real possibility. There were obvious obstacles, of course. Some of the cosmetic surgical procedures couldn't be undone, but some could. Once again, he decided to have his breast implants removed from his already deeply scarred chest. He also felt confident enough to take a second run at amending his birth certificate, this time changing it from Laura Jensen, female, back to Walt Heyer, male. He found an attorney who suggested that a strongly worded letter from a doctor attesting to Heyer's maleness would be enough to convince the court to restore his birth record to its original form.

But once again, the complexities of his dual life made that seemingly simple request immensely complex. At the time, Heyer says California law did not acknowledge the possibility that someone would want to restore their gender once it had been changed. Changing it back would require proof that the reversal had been done surgically, which Heyer had not done, and could not afford to do. And after everything he'd already been through, he was not willing to risk more surgery. For the time being, his effort to legally become Walt Heyer, male, stalled.

But he began to change his gender identity on other documents that offered fewer hurdles, and which did not require a birth certificate. He registered to vote as Walt Heyer. The Social Security Administration was willing to change his name and gender as well. So was the California Department of Motor Vehicles, and he became Walter Heyer again on his driver's license. He gradually reclaimed his birth identity one document at a time.

When the time came to change his US passport, Heyer hit a roadblock. It was a particularly difficult rejection for him. A year before, he'd traveled to visit his son at an Air Force base in England. While his children understood his gender issues, he'd never before presented himself as Laura Jensen to either of his children. But when Heyer and his son were stopped at a base guardhouse and asked for credentials, he'd presented his passport. It was issued in the name of Laura Jensen, with a photograph of Heyer dressed as that female persona. The incident pained him, because he could tell his son was embarrassed and angry for the rest of their visit. That had given Heyer's effort to change his passport back to his male persona an intensely personal motivation.

He had approached the clerk at the downtown San Francisco passport office with some trepidation, but by then was armed with what he hoped would be persuasive evidence—along with his passport application and a photo of himself as Walt, he wielded his voter registration, doctors' affidavits, driver's license, and his Social Security card. All of them listed him as Walter Heyer, male.

But when the clerk researched his Social Security records, he found Walter Heyer listed as female. Because of the mismatching information, the clerk told Heyer the only way he could issue a passport was to list him as Walter Heyer, female.

"How crazy is this?" he recalled thinking years later. "Destroying my real identity after surgery had been so easy. Restoring it back was proving to be seemingly impossible."

Disappointed, nearly distraught, Heyer calmed himself and asked to see a supervisor, an older woman. He remembers explaining the situation to her in a quavering voice, struggling to keep his breathing calm. He laid out his documents and began telling his story, explaining why the passport change was terribly important to him. He was near tears, he recalls, when the supervisor made a decision almost certainly shaped by handling other complicated cases in the San Francisco office of the California Department of Motor Vehicles. She said, "Sweetie, I'm going to take care of this for you."

Again, Heyer remembers the moment as one where God intervened on his behalf. He refers to the passport office supervisor as "an angel," and believes Jesus was guiding her the moment she decided to restore his passport paperwork to list him as Walter Heyer, male. His birth certificate would, for the time being, show him as a female. But now he had a valid US passport that represented him as the man he now felt himself to be.

Living with the Thompsons, and with a new job arranged, Heyer approached the end of 1996 with high hopes. Chief among his reasons: Kaycee, the woman for whom he was falling fast, had invited him to her employer's Christmas party.

They had known each other for several years at that point. Kaycee had seen Walt as Laura only once, from across a Mexican restaurant during a birthday party for their mutual friend, Cathy, from whom Laura Jensen was renting a room. They never met and never spoke. "I kept bugging my friend to meet her roommate Laura," Kaycee says. "Finally, she said, 'You know I need to tell you something.' So, with Walt's permission she told me about his struggle with his gender. So then, when I met Walt, I met Walt."

With their mutual friends, Kaycee and Walt Heyer began getting together for occasional meals. A friendship developed. Kaycee's first impressions? "Mostly it was compassion for this man who seemed to have gone off-track somewhere and was trying to find his way back," she says.

Kaycee and Heyer began corresponding by email, a medium in which she was comfortable, but he was not. But he'd scrounged enough money to buy a used laptop and signed on with a dial-up wireless Internet service that allowed him to send and receive emails anywhere in the Bay Area. He often wrote to her from coffee shops and restaurants during his lunch hour, even from his car. It felt like a running daily conversation.

The friendship grew organically, through shared meals and long conversations. She considered him a close friend, but not necessarily anything more. But as a child of an alcoholic parent,

Kaycee says she was tired of being "the sick one" in her adult relationships. Plus, even though her marriage of thirteen years ended in divorce, she was ready to be married again after seven years of living the single life.

At the time, she was doing web marketing for a large Silicon Valley tech company that was flying high then, but no longer exists. The Christmas party invitation was no small deal to Heyer, both because this was no ordinary party and because the invitation signaled a willingness on Kaycee's part to consider him more than just a friend. "They must have spent millions on that party," she recalls. "They had acrobats. They had stilt walkers. They had incredible food."

Kaycee later recalled her attraction to Heyer in a chapter she wrote for Heyer's memoir. She gravitated toward people who had struggle intensely, whose lives bore the scars and accumulated wisdom of hard-fought experience. "I liked being with people who had experienced gut-wrenching pain and done the hard work of therapy like I was doing. They were real, and they didn't make me feel like I was the 'odd' one."

Once, when they were seeing each other as friends, Kaycee had challenged him as he fretted about his ability to continue to hold his Walt persona together. "What's the matter?" she said. "Don't you think your God is big enough to heal you?" He recalls the moment as one where she seemed to know him better than he knew himself, and as the moment when he stopped having any urge to live as Laura Jensen.

In Heyer, she says she saw a man who'd survived the "tragic and unforeseen consequences of earlier choices." And she was impressed by his deep commitment—a commitment she shared—to Jesus Christ. Plus, she had always found him easy to be with and enjoyed his company and sense of humor. But she also understood his fragility. She worried that dating him or in any way leading him on could involve tragic consequences if things didn't work out. She wrote, "I did not want to inflict that kind of harm on my precious friend."

She'd once made a list of traits she wanted in an ideal partner. It stretched to thirty-five items. Among them were some basics such as "pleasant attitude" and "laughs at himself" and "gets over arguments easily."

But she was conscious of her shortcomings as well. She'd struggled with codependency issues and was aware of the importance of entering into a relationship on equal footing. It bothered her that despite his meager income, Heyer often paid for the lunches they shared and that he usually drove a long distance to meet her for those meals rather than the other way around. Things felt out of balance, so one day she drove twenty-five miles to bring Heyer a burrito for lunch as he labored over a truck at the automotive shop where he'd been working. Heyer took that kindness as an encouraging sign.

Heyer picked Kaycee up for the Christmas party, nervous and uncertain about being out with a woman for the first time in fifteen years. Since his marriage ended, he'd avoided any sort of romantic notions because his life was in such disarray. "Switching back and forth between Walt and Laura made it impossible to even consider having other relationships," he recalls. "My view of myself through those years was that I was on the trash heap of humanity—someone no one would ever want."

In recent years, he'd focused instead on staying sober. His social life involved his church and his AA meetings. Kaycee's assurance that they were going to the Christmas party as "just buddies" was a mixed blessing. It relieved some of the pressure and awkwardness, but it also seemed less of a commitment than he had hoped. Nonetheless enamored, he pressed on, inviting her to dinner the following month to celebrate her birthday. She accepted, and he recalls that they had a wonderful time. A friendship ignited by tragedy was clearly evolving into something far more joyful.

When the dinner was over, Heyer paid the bill and stood up to leave. Kaycee remained seated.

"Do you know what you just did?" he recalls her asking with a smile.

Heyer, like so many who struggle with gender issues, was confused, and assumed the worst. What had he done?

"You just did a date!"

In their shared laughter Heyer detected the unfamiliar sound of hope.

———————

Five years after first meeting Kaycee, Heyer began charting the progress of their budding romance like a teenager, marking his calendar with the dates of the first movie during which they held hands, their first hug, and their first kiss. By Valentine's Day that year, they had graduated to dinner and dancing. Two days later, they drove to Los Angeles so Heyer could introduce Kaycee to his once-estranged daughter and Heyer's mother.

"A miracle was unfolding in this area of my life that I had thought was beyond redemption," he later wrote in his book *A Transgender's Faith*. "There was an undeniable explosion of love. You cannot explain it, but you sure can feel it, and there is nothing like it."

Kaycee had been doing a little bookkeeping of her own. She'd run Heyer through her potential partner checklist and was delighted to find that he fulfilled thirty-four of her thirty-five wishes. The only criteria he didn't meet? He didn't ski.

The visit with Heyer's daughter and mother went well, and Heyer says his daughter leaned toward Kaycee's ear as they were preparing to leave. She whispered, "Thanks for taking care of my dad," and in those words Heyer heard another trace of hope. After so many years of anger and alienation from his daughter, Heyer allowed himself to believe that someday their relationship could be fully healed.

The couple continued to intensify their own relationship, and to consult with Christian counselors. Where they were heading was obvious to those who knew them. Roy Thompson began hinting that the family's Pleasanton backyard might be a fine place for a wedding.

Heyer proposed to Kaycee on Easter Sunday morning, just months after their friendship took a turn toward something more serious. She accepted, and they set a wedding date of May 18, 1997. About a hundred people gathered in the Thompson's back yard to witness it. Thompson conducted the ceremony alongside Kaycee's pastor. Jeff Farrar, who'd accepted the task of counseling Laura Jensen so long ago and rallied his congregation into a support group, stood as Heyer's best man. Their mutual friend Cathy, just two months away from dying of colon cancer, was there as well. They were joined by the once-anonymous prayer team that Farrar had put together, as well as the elders who once asked Heyer not to attend their services anymore.

"My struggle with identity was over and a new life began," Heyer declared in one of the final chapters of his book. "I am the man God created me to be."

Not exactly, of course. His long-ago surgery in Trinidad had stranded him in a physical limbo, and he embarked on his new marriage as a man with a vagina. Heyer won't discuss the intimate details of his marital life with Kaycee, understandably saying some things need to remain private. According to Kaycee's written account in Heyer's book, their discussion of their sexual limitations unfolded in a simple, oblique metaphor.

She asked him if he was bothered by the fact that she was taller. He said no, and asked her if she was bothered by the fact that he was shorter.

She said she was not.

"In that same simplicity of heart, with God's grace, and through our mutual unconditional love, other differences that might have mattered a great deal have mattered not at all."

When Heyer told her he was embarrassed by the many scars on his chest from his many breast implant and removal surgeries, she told him this: "All people have scars. Yours are just on the outside."

23

Surprise

The city of Surprise, Arizona, just outside Phoenix, looks like so many bedroom communities scattered throughout the Southwest, a tidy collection of gated housing developments, artificial water features, and planned commercial districts that might have been dropped whole from outer space onto this available spot in the American Sun Belt. There's a Panera restaurant there, and that's where Walt Heyer chose to meet for one last interview about life since his passage through Trinidad and his difficult "detransition" back into life as a happily married man. Despite having shared details of his struggles in intimate detail, he was reluctant to meet at his nearby home—perhaps because he knew a lot of people don't much like him or what he has to say these days about gender confirmation surgery and regret.

It was hard to identify Heyer and Kaycee, now his wife of twenty-two years, among the other older couples enjoying a late January lunch. The tipoff was that they were the only ones seated on the same side of their booth. They waved me over and into the bench seat that faced them.

More than two decades sober, Heyer was wearing a plaid shirt and jeans, his hair a bright white wave atop his head. He's small and his face is delicate, with a surgicallyrefined and feminized nose, eyes behind black-framed glasses, and no apparent beard. They're living in Surprise, he explained, because the doctor who for the past three years has been treating him for esophageal cancer is based here. He was scheduled for another endoscopy procedure in a few days, his eighteenth, and has lost count of the number of elective surgeries to which he has subjected his body.

"I don't even want to think about it," he said. "It's exhausting."

Despite occasional pain and difficulty eating and sleeping,

he was for the moment cancer-free and looking forward to relocating someplace with "ten acres with a view."

"Yeah, with perfect weather and under $300,000," Kaycee added with a laugh.

She was dressed casually as well, but her kind and open face concealed an assertive protectiveness toward her husband. They laugh easily and appear to be equal and amiable partners who, like many couples their age, often complete each other's sentences.

Heyer began the conversation with a story that suggested his mind remains an unreliable narrator of his experiences before, during, and after his 1983 gender confirmation surgery. "The thing to understand is that during that period of my life my brain felt like it was in a Mixmaster," he said. "Even now, trying to remember and put events into a logical order is hard to do."

As proof, he said he'd recently received an email from a transgender friend named Lori, whom he'd first met during his time at The Roadrunner bar in San Francisco's Tenderloin District. In that email, Lori reminded him that she and another friend who'd already been through the surgery had actually accompanied him on his second trip to Trinidad, the one where he followed through, surrendered himself to Dr. Stanley Biber's surgical skills, and emerged from the operating room as Laura Jensen. Heyer made no mention in his memoir of having had travel companions during that trip because, he said, he simply did not remember it.

Lori apparently had followed Heyer's recent career, including the launch of his website for those experiencing what he calls "sex-change regret," his self-published memoir *A Transgender's Faith*, and his other testimonial books that often include stories of people like him who eventually came to regret their gender transition through hormone therapy and surgical intervention. His persistent theme is to urge a more cautious approach to treatment of those who consider themselves transgender, and he said Lori wanted him to know that her experience with him in Trinidad more than three decades earlier had profoundly affected the trajectory of her life.

It's worth noting that Heyer provided only a redacted version of Lori's email, and declined to offer any contact information for her to verify his account of their communication. But his candor about his own memory lapse and the details she shared in the redacted version—the three of them landing at the Denver airport and their long drive to Trinidad, their walk to Mt. San Rafael on the day of his surgery, her nervous wait with the other companion while Biber did the surgery—suggested that Heyer is simply trying to protect the privacy of a friend.

In the truncated version of the email that Heyer shared, Lori recalled being shown into the hospital room for a first post-op visit with the recovering Laura Jensen. Lori asked her still-groggy friend if she was in pain. The reply, she recalled, was "elephant." Lori asked for clarification and got a fuller answer—"Elephant sitting on me"—that convinced her Biber had *not* removed his patient's sense of humor.

Lori also told Heyer she was in his hospital room the day a nurse arrived to change the dressing covering his new vagina. She said she got a bit light-headed during the big reveal, and nearly fainted when "with forceps she began pulling what was yard after yard of pus laden gauze. I thought it would never end! Pulling and pulling and ... the blood drained from my face, the cold sweat poured from me, my heart beating wildly in my chest ... a full-blown panic attack."

She remembered that her knees buckled, and that she grabbed the bed rail to steady herself. "It was right there in a split second, my entire life changed," she wrote. "In that moment the Lord [that] I was so angry with let me know I would never, ever have that surgery! I had no idea what my future held. But it wouldn't be SRS![26] Little did either of us know that your Ministry started decades ago ... in the early '80s ... in the middle of nowhere!"

The ministry to which Lori refers is the one Heyer says he launched with no expectations in about 2008 when he registered the domain name sexchangeregret.com. By his account, things snowballed from there.

"When I started the website, I just wondered if anybody else had regrets. I said maybe I'm the only one and I was willing to accept that," he explained.

About 700 people visited the website during its first year, and he said perhaps only five of those actually reached out to Heyer. But word got around, and he began doing interviews with people curious about the topic. "I'm doing little radio shows where these people are operating from their bedrooms, very minuscule things," he recalled. But then, in April 2015, the Caitlyn Jenner transition became front-page news. That was the year he also republished his 2006 memoir *Trading My Sorrows* as *A Transgender's Faith*.

"When Jenner hit, I'm on Rush Limbaugh, I'm on CNN, I did forty radio and TV shows in five days," he recalled. "I'm doing shows in the UK, I'm on the BBC, and I'm authoring articles" about what he considers the risk of ignoring the psychological underpinnings of self-identified transgender men and women before prescribing hormone and surgical treatment. Those articles often appear in The Federalist, a right-leaning web magazine founded in 2013 that focuses on culture, politics, and religion, but which does not disclose its source of funding.

Heyer's website had more than 350,000 unique visitors in 2015, and he began getting invitations to speak at conferences, some as far away as Australia and Spain. He says more people began contacting him through the website, telling their stories, asking questions, sharing their uncertainties. His other self-published books began selling better, including 2011's *Paper Genders* and 2013's *Gender, Lies and Suicide: A Whistleblower Speaks Out*. In a self-published 2018 book, *Trans Life Survivors*, he shares thirty regret stories (without using real names or identifying details) from people who he says have contacted him. He wrote it, he explains in the introduction, "because I want others to catch a glimpse of the raw emotions and experiences of people who are harmed by the grand—and dangerous—experiment of cross-sex hormones and surgical reaffirming procedures."

Heyer eventually enlisted Kaycee to help keep up with the emails, and between his late-night esophageal pain and the crush of correspondence, he said he often finds himself at his computer at 4 a.m. "digging into the emails so I can clear the inbox out before the next day starts." By March 2019, emails to him generated an automatic response: "I'm doing my best to answer each and every email, but there is a chance that I won't be able to answer due to the volume of email I receive each day. Thanks for your understanding."

All that has established Heyer firmly as a willing antagonist to those who advocate for transgender rights, and who accept the view that hormone treatment and gender confirmation surgery are effective treatments for gender dysphoria. He explained that his decision to play that role is based mostly on the high suicide rate among the transgender population.

"That right there is the core of my issue," he said, pushing away his lunch plate. "By taking a troubled person and giving them hormones and cutting off body parts and rearranging them, you've nailed where I get upset. Especially today when they're trying to legislate anyone from having access to psychotherapy if they represent themselves as transgender. They must be fearful they're going to uncover a comorbidity that's going to show this whole thing is a mass fraud in terms of people who self-identify as a transgender."

His goal, he insisted, is not to deny access to hormone therapy and surgery for those who truly suffer from gender dysphoria. And he conceded that there are real cases out there for which that prescription can mean relief. But based on what he's heard from those who contact him—a self-selecting group, he admitted—therapists and clinicians are too quick to settle on that course of treatment, and too seldom consider psychological roots such as childhood sexual abuse that he feels can lead someone to that crossroads. "I'm not trying to kill the whole thing," he said. "I'm just trying to prevent unnecessary surgical procedures and hormone therapies and putting people through this."

Heyer said he knows of some clinics where ample care is taken to ensure that all factors are taken into account before diagnosis and treatment. "Some of them have a rigid protocol, and they look for comorbidities, they look for dissociative disorders, they look for bipolar disorder, they look for schizophrenia. They look for all these other issues. Was the person sexually abused? I say never do hormones and surgery on someone who has been sexually abused, because we see an extremely high prevalence of that in people who contact us."

In the increasingly polarized political and social climate since the 2016 presidential election, Heyer's critics often accuse him of using his platform to stir anti-trans sentiment, or to promote himself and his books at the expense of an already vulnerable population. "People say, 'Well you're out there rattling the bushes,'" he said. "No, I just have a website so people who are struggling know where to go. Right now, this is probably the most rewarding and the most demanding and the most exhausting thing we've ever done."

It's also the least financially rewarding, both he and Kaycee agree. Through the website and during personal appearances, they may sell fifty or sixty books a month to a target audience they realize is only a tiny fraction of the reading public.

"And that's a good month!" Kaycee said. "We've depleted our retirement account to pay the bills."

Heyer laughs. "Kaycee just finished the taxes and I said, 'How'd we do?' She said, 'We're $300 over the poverty limit.'"

"We've had people write to him and say 'I know you're getting rich off this ... '" Kaycee said.

Heyer shook his head. "I mean, that is fantasy."

He's not the first person to play the antagonist's role. His story echoes that of the late Perry Desmond, a drag queen and former New Orleans prostitute who in 1978 published an autobiography titled *Perry: A Transformed Transsexual: A Life-Long Search for Identity*, in which he tells of a Christian conversion similar to Heyer's after undergoing male-to-female surgery. After his conversion, Desmond returned to living as a man until his death nine years later.

Including Heyer in these pages is guaranteed to invite scorn from those who consider him a pariah. They group him with such outspoken critics of the transgender movement as Paul R. McHugh, the former Johns Hopkins Hospital psychiatrist-in-chief who convinced the hospital to stop doing gender confirmation surgeries in 1979; and Ryan T. Anderson, a Heritage Foundation fellow and author of the book *When Harry Became Sally*, which "exposes the contrast between the media's sunny depiction of gender fluidity and the often sad reality of living with gender dysphoria." Heyer says he has appeared at events featuring both McHugh and Anderson. He considers both to be friends and he relies heavily on McHugh's opinions as the basis of his own. For that reason, it's important to understand McHugh's arguments against surgery as a treatment for gender dysphoria.

Paul McHugh became head psychiatrist at Johns Hopkins Hospital in 1975 and believed, based on his own experiences, that the surgical fix for gender dysphoria was misguided. He set out to challenge what he considered flawed assumptions. At the center of his thinking was a simple suspicion: He wasn't persuaded by transgender patients who told him that they were happy and contented after their surgeries.

"The post-surgical subjects struck me as caricatures of women," he wrote in a 2004 essay published in the flagship magazine of the nonprofit Institute on Religion and Public Life. "They wore high heels, copious makeup, and flamboyant clothing; they spoke about how they found themselves able to give vent to their natural inclinations for peace, domesticity, and gentleness—but their large hands, prominent Adam's apples, and thick facial features were incongruous (and would become more so as they aged). Women psychiatrists whom I sent to talk with them would intuitively see through the disguise and the exaggerated postures. 'Gals know gals,' one said to me, 'and that's a guy.'"

McHugh also relied on the research work of colleague Jon Meyer, who had concluded that while few patients who underwent the surgery regretted it, their psychological condition wasn't much changed as a result. "The hope that they would emerge now from their emotional difficulties to flourish psychologically had not been fulfilled," McHugh wrote in 2004.

Meyer had concluded, too, that the mental disorders driving those who pursue surgery fell into two different groups: 1) Guilt-ridden homosexual men who saw transition as a way to resolve their conflicts over homosexuality by allowing themselves to behave sexually as heterosexual females; and 2) Mostly older heterosexual and bisexual men who found intense sexual arousal by cross-dressing as females. Their decision to pursue surgery, McHugh claimed, was because they were "eager to add more verisimilitude to their costumes."

McHugh interpreted Meyer's research to mean that it was wrong to provide surgery to those people, and that doing so was "to collaborate with a mental disorder rather than to treat it." He also has said that "policy makers and the media are doing no favors either to the public or the transgendered by treating their confusions as a right in need of defending rather than as a mental disorder that deserves understanding, treatment, and prevention."

By ending the elite Johns Hopkins program in 1979, McHugh spooked many similar university-based programs that at the time were offering the surgery. They began getting out of the business about the time Stanley Biber's reputation was growing, ultimately bringing Walter Heyer, Claudine Griggs, and thousands of patients like them to Trinidad.

Decades later, Heyer clearly considers McHugh an inspiration, and Johns Hopkins's recent reinstatement of its gender confirmation surgery program a betrayal of McHugh's long-ago decision. He claims the reversal was done because wealthy alumni sympathetic to the transgender cause fell under the sway of liberal policymakers, Hollywood, and the mainstream media. They demanded the program's reinstatement, Heyer said, though not for legitimate medical reasons.

"They still can't prove that transgenders exist medically,"

Heyer claims. "That's still a fact of life. There's no way to prove that a transgender exists. So they go ahead and do 'gender-affirming surgery.' That term gives us a clue as to what this is about. They want to affirm your gender. They don't say that we have medical proof that you need hormones and surgery, they just want to affirm whatever you want. This is where we are today. It's all about affirm, affirm, affirm."

Heyer predicted that "we're going to see this whole transgender thing in the next five to ten years totally collapse upon itself."

It's hard not to weigh Heyer's dire prediction against some of the other statements he made during our various conversations, which suggest he gives credence to conspiracy theories and sometimes discredited conservative tropes. He believes billionaire George Soros is a Marxist who has funded his liberal agenda to the tune of hundreds of millions of dollars, making him "the titular head of the LGBT." He also applies that same label to former President Barack Obama, who he says "appointed 250 LGBT activists to infiltrate and push the transgender agenda." Heyer believes many of the wealthy people funding the gay-rights movement "are homosexual or transgender, and we have Soros at the top of the list.... They want to destroy the moral fabric of society, of the Church, and if you can destroy gender, then you can destroy the basis of man-woman marriage, and then in due time destroy the foundation of society, which is the male-female family and spawning of offspring. So George Soros is totally against God and family."

The LGBTQ community of "sexual activists," Heyer believes, have "done more to destroy lives than any other single group in history."

Heyer often points to high-profile cases of "detransitioners," people who transitioned into the opposite sex only to later change their minds. He includes in that group Mike Penner, a former *Los Angeles Times* sportswriter who publicly announced his transition from male to female in a 2007 column that read in part: "I am a transsexual sportswriter. It has taken more than forty years, a million tears and hundreds of hours of soul-wrenching therapy for me to work up the courage to type those words...."

When you reach the point when one gender causes heartache and unbearable discomfort, and the other brings more joy and fulfillment than you ever imagined possible, it shouldn't take two tons of bricks to fall in order to know what to do."

The journalist lived and wrote as Christine Daniels for more than a year, even chronicling his transition experience in a blog for the paper. But less than a year later, he abruptly resumed writing as Mike Penner and committed suicide in November 2009 at age fifty-two.

Heyer cites, too, the case of Alexis Arquette, of the famous Hollywood acting dynasty, who straddled genders for much of her post-adolescent life before reverting to her previous identity as Robert Arquette while dying of an HIV-related infection in 2016. Heyer focuses on comments Arquette apparently made to a fellow drag performer friend during her final days that "gender is bullshit." Arquette reportedly said that "putting on a dress doesn't biologically change anything. Nor does a sex change." And she concluded that "sex-reassignment is physically impossible. All you can do is adopt these superficial characteristics, but the biology will never change."[27]

Heyer also focuses on vague comments about transition regrets made by former tennis star Dr. Renee Richards, whose transition from male to female was revealed in 1976 when she signed up to play in a women's tournament and she suddenly became a public figure. But while Richards was quite clear in a 2007 *New York Times* article that she did not regret having the surgery, Heyer emphasizes the story's headline ("The Lady Regrets") and comments she made that suggest some disappointment with the results, including the statement, "Better to be an intact man functioning with one-hundred percent capacity for everything than to be a transsexual woman who is an imperfect woman," and her wish that "if there were a drug, some voodoo, any kind of mind-altering magic remedy to keep the man intact, that would have been preferable, but there wasn't."

Heyer, who studied psychology at the University of California, Santa Cruz, and has worked as a professional counselor but who is not a psychiatrist or psychologist, also believes many trans men are suffering from the condition known as *autogynephilia*, which is a theoretical condition describing a male's propensity to be sexually aroused by the thought of himself as a female. Heyer believes autogynephilia underpins transvesticism and some forms of male-to-female transsexualism. He theorizes that various traumas in Caitlyn Jenner's past drove her decision to transition from his life as the male decathlon champion in the 1976 Summer Olympics—a paragon of manhood—into a high-profile, high-glam female celebrated on the cover of *Vanity Fair*. Those traumas include a car accident that claimed the life of her younger brother Burt and her brother's female friend shortly after Jenner's Olympic triumph, as well as a February 2015 fatal accident in Malibu that killed sixty-nine-year-old Kim Howe.[28]

Heyer points out that Jenner spoke openly about her thoughts of suicide during a now-famous post-transition television interview with Diane Sawyer on April 24, 2015. He cites it as proof that the psychological traumas that lie beneath the impulse to transition into another gender often are never addressed, as happened with his own early therapist Paul Walker.

"Suicide—that's pretty critical stuff," he said of the Jenner-Sawyer interview. "And they blew right over it. They didn't focus on the suicide discussion that Jenner brought forward. It was like blowing through a red light. Sawyer should have stopped and said, 'Tell me more about this. How did you get to that point of thinking?' And Sawyer did not have Jenner talk about the three vehicle deaths that Jenner was involved in. Those are traumatic and emotionally disturbing and cause people to have difficulty when they're not totally dealt with."

Heyer said he sees a familiar pattern when transgender people contact him about their regrets. "When I sit with people and talk to them, that's when they break down and start talking about how they ended up where they are. [Jenner] having been involved in three deaths as a result of car accidents is pretty critical. And then the fact that suicide was discussed in a pretty direct way, I'm watching this saying, 'Nobody's discussing this. Look at this.' I mean, it's amazing to me."

No one should be surprised that Heyer, his books, and his ongoing sexchangeregret.com crusade are given little credence by experts and those within the LGBTQ and transgender community. They correctly point out that his experience is far from typical, and his assumption that nearly all transgender men and women will, like him, eventually regret their decision to transition is fatally flawed. But the story of his tortured journey through decades of gender confusion, hormones and surgery, and mental illness is no less valid because of that criticism, and to ignore his story is a failure to acknowledge the complex nature of gender identity and the vast unknowns yet to be understood. His case may be extreme and well outside the norm, and his interpretation of his experience skewed by a religious and political agenda, but it's important to consider alongside those of others who have walked the same difficult road. It's just as important to recognize that he is not now and never was gender dysphoric. He was misdiagnosed as such, which complicated his life in countless ways. But it's also risky to mistake his strong and heartfelt opinions about gender dysphoria for expertise.

Transgender historian Susan Stryker believes that most of those who eventually regret transitioning or having gender confirmation surgery are people who got bad counseling when they needed it most. She says Heyer's experience with Paul Walker, his first counselor, is a prime example. "Walker is one of those people who was a WPATH tried-and-true kind of guy who prided himself as an expert, a gatekeeper, a decider, a decision-maker. But Paul was gay and saw himself as 'I really get these trans people because we're all fellow travelers and I'm one of the cool ones.' He was very invested in his role as expert on gender dysphoria and he did a lot of good for a lot of people. But he was kind of like the arrogant liberal who thinks he knows what's best for everyone. I'm sorry that that aspect of Walker's worldview had a bad intersection with Mr. Regret."

But she's quick to add that regret like Heyer's is quite uncommon. "Yes, there will be some people who have regrets, no question about it," she says. "I tend to think they're people who were promised the world and didn't get the world, or people who have ambivalence."

As simplistic as it sounds, she says some people simply have trouble making decisions. "I have friends like this. They do this thing, and they agonize over it, then they go, 'Why did I do that thing?' There's a kind of neurosis involved."

Others like Heyer who arrive at regret through some sort of religious experience feel the need to set right a decision they made during a period of their life when they felt out of control. "People are diverse, and I'm sorry [Heyer] has regrets," Stryker says. "But from the literature I've read, people like that are a minor proportion of the population, and they receive an outsized level of attention. And then it gets weaponized and politicized."

In fact, because of a prevailing climate of intolerance in 2019, Stryker advised me to not include Heyer's story in this book. She cites the Trump Administration's ban on transgender men and woman in the US military, as well as a resurgent controversy in Great Britain over the Gender Recognition Act of 2004, which enables transsexual people to apply to receive a Gender Recognition Certificate. That document shows that a person has satisfied the criteria for legal recognition in the acquired gender, but does not correct or provide a new birth certificate. In November 2017, the Scottish government reassessed the law and found it "out of date" and its requirements on those applying for a gender change "intrusive and onerous." A reform effort began, and naturally, controversy ensued.

"People have their stories, and you want those meaty, complicated stories," Stryker says of my decision to include Heyer's story. "But some stories are better told than others. Not that you want to censor anything, but at a certain moment telling a certain story in a certain context might have unintended consequences. Which is not to say don't do it. But it's a very inflamed topic right now."

She's joined in that opinion by Sarah-Wade Smith, a mid-sixty-year-old trans woman and Tennessee native, who describes Heyer as "the sort of person transphobic people will use to try to invalidate my identity as a woman. Because his transition was impulsive and later regretted, then Claudine Griggs's transition and mine must be equally invalid, and therefore we're just men in dresses."

There's genuine concern in Stryker's voice as she adds that while Heyer's story may speak directly to people who are struggling to understand the transgender experience, it doesn't do so in a productive way. "A lot of cisgender people have that, 'What if I have sex change surgery and it's the wrong thing?' fear," she says. "Or if it's a guy, they're saying, 'What if I cut my dick off and am sorry?' So the people who do have regrets then become poster children for the anxieties of other people, when in fact most trans people—the vast majority in my experience—are satisfied with the decision that they made."

She's careful to add the same cautionary note that so many transgender men and women do when discussing the value of gender confirmation surgery. "It's not that they don't say, 'Yeah, I wish things had worked out a little better,' or 'This doesn't really work that well.' Or whatever. But there's still an acceptance in the peace of the choice that you've made, even if the surgical outcome is not a 100-plus."

Heyer said it was time for him and Kaycee to go. He hadn't slept well the night before, and recovering from those rough nights of pain isn't so easy to do since he turned eighty years old. He offered to send a copy of his latest book and accepted a previous one of mine in trade.

In a follow-up email a few days later, he voiced a surprising take on his long struggle with mental illness. In *A Transgender's Faith*, he wrote about his dissociative-disorder diagnosis as a revelation that helped explain his often extreme gender confusion. But he also said he wrote that book in 2004, and in hindsight believes he might write parts of it differently today— including accepting that diagnosis as absolute.

"The diagnosis of dissociative disorder was not supported by all the therapists," he wrote. "And the therapist who I feel provided the most effective psychotherapy never believed the diagnosis was accurate."

True, he felt the word dissociation accurately described the feeling he got when switching between the personalities of Walt Heyer and Laura Jensen. He could feel himself psychologically distancing himself from that confused young man in the purple dress being feminized and fussed over by his grandmother. Plus, he wrote, "I liked having a diagnosis to tell my friends."

But all these years later, he tells a more nuanced and less clear-cut version of that psychological explanation. He was out of work and money in the late 1980s, and he had applied for disability support from Medicaid. "The State of California had a PhD do an extensive evaluation of me over a period of one week," he wrote. "I told him I was told I had a dissociative disorder. He thought because I was familiar with what a dissociative disorder looked like, I 'acted out' a dissociative disorder but didn't actually have one."

But Heyer said the therapist was sure that Heyer had little or no chance of finding a job, and so approved his application even though he remained unconvinced that the diagnosis was accurate. The Medicaid checks began arriving a few months later, and that was that.

Still, Heyer wonders. Was that the problem? Or something else? Either way, he's clean and sober, and the gender switching has stopped, and he and Kaycee have built a stable life together that he clearly cherishes. In the Panera parking lot, Walt Heyer—the demonized but unapologetic provocateur to the LGBTQ community—offered me an awkward hug and three pats on the back.

"You know what the three pats mean, right?" he said. "It means you're not gay."

I wasn't exactly sure how to respond. But then he laughed. He was still smiling a minute later when he recalled the words of a former pastor that underpin his relentless drive in recent years to make sure his story gets told.

"At my age I have one foot on the dock and one foot on the boat," he said. "And the boat is leaving."

24
An Era Ends

The waiting area of surgeon Marci Bowers's private office in Burlingame, California, is clearing out at the end of a spring 2018 workday. In some ways, the office where Bowers spends her non-surgery hours these days feels more like a counseling office in which the conversation among the visitors ranges from depression to divorce to local support groups. A father waits for his transgender daughter to emerge from the examination rooms behind a closed door, and when she does, they step out onto the city's Lorton Avenue, which is dotted with upscale boutiques and restaurants about a ten-minute drive from San Francisco International Airport.

The last person remaining is an effusive writing teacher at City College of San Francisco who has been entertaining us and Bowers's receptionist in the waiting room with observations such as "making vaginas is a real art" and how the process is "like origami, turning a 2D surface into 3D." She's waiting for her friend who emerges a few minutes later wearing skinny jeans that move as one with her rail-thin figure.

The friend is accompanied by Bowers, who is wearing a stylish black outfit and matching boots that end just below her knees. The surgeon looks tired after a long day, maybe a little wary. Her handshake is gentle, almost limp, and she gathers her things for a short drive to the Japanese restaurant she has chosen for the nearly three-hour conversation to come. Her already long day is about to get longer, and she's moving gingerly after a recent skiing accident that left her with a fractured vertebrae. She also has to be up for an early surgery the following day.

Still, she graciously insists she's eager to talk about her relationship with Stanley Biber, her years in Trinidad, those who decry what she does for a living, and why she decided to end

Trinidad's forty-one-year run as "the sex-change capital of the world" by moving from there to here.

Commitment was never really the problem. Bowers had moved to Trinidad intending to continue Stanley Biber's surgical legacy, and had made plenty of choices that suggested her intention to stay. She and partner Carol Cometto were a familiar couple around town during Bowers's final years there, and were instrumental in helping two trans women open a five-bedroom recovery house called Morning Glow. They envisioned a post-op refuge where Bowers's patients could rest and recuperate from their surgeries among people who'd just been through the same physical and emotional trauma.

The development of that facility, encouraged by but not financially backed by Bowers, was the focus of a documentary film by Jay Hodges and PJ Raval called simply *Trinidad*. It premiered on the Showtime network in 2009 and focused on the efforts of two of Bowers's gender confirmation surgery patients, Sabrina Marcus and Dr. Laura Ellis, to renovate one of Trinidad's Victorian houses into a sort of post-op bed-and-breakfast. Filmmakers Hodges and Raval aimed high, hoping to chronicle "the universal struggle for self-expression" among the trans women by using their backstories to explore their gender experiences.

Instead, the filmmakers ended up chronicling a slow-motion train wreck that foreshadowed a critical transition for the town of Trinidad itself. As *Trinidad* vividly depicts, the Morning Glow project faltered as renovation deadlines went unmet, personalities clashed, and financing became burdensome. In the end, the film's unpleasant denouement shows the renovation project on the brink of collapse after a year of effort, with Bowers growing impatient and disillusioned, and Ellis, its primary financier, moving off to Alabama to start a new life there.

By then, other signs around town were pointing to trouble. The live-and-let-live attitude that Biber had cultivated in Trinidad was never universal, and from time to time a politician or letter writer to the local newspaper would lament the town's reputation as a surgical crossroads for transgender pilgrims. There was a flurry of such talk in 2005, just two years into Bowers's tenure, when fundamentalist Protestant organizations such as the Trinidad Ministerial Alliance and Focus on the Family in nearby Colorado Springs decided to make it a cause. Their chest-thumping led to a June 2005 headline in the *Pueblo Chieftain* reading "Trinidad's Clergy Fight 'Sex Change Capital' Label."

Those sentiments were countered by the Reverend Bob Hagan, pastor of the Catholic Holy Trinity Parish in downtown Trinidad, who told the filmmakers, "I believe the gender reassignment process is an area where it's very difficult to come up with a one-size-fits-all morality. We need to realize that people are unique in their sexuality ... and they may not fit neatly into preconceived categories .... It's very important that we not fail in love."

But the debate seemed suddenly renewed nearly four decades after Biber first began the conversation. Bowers expected a certain level of concern as she moved into town and assumed Biber's duties at the hospital, and by all accounts she handled that concern with patience and resolve to forge ahead. But as the media spotlight intensified, so did the talk. Not everyone was pleased about that.

Cometto, who now manages the Tire Shop liquor and wine store on the city's Main Street owned by Bowers's patient and former Trinidad City Council member Michelle Miles, was Bowers's romantic partner for most of her years in Trinidad. She insists that most people in town welcomed and appreciated the new surgeon. "I get my customers coming in asking, 'You think Marci will ever come back?' And I'm like, 'No.' But it was just a handful of people that made the difference. People like the guy that was president of the golf association and on the board at the hospital that said, 'Oh, all right, we don't want that.' So, it wasn't the community. It was just a select few people that have control over this town at some point. And Marci just couldn't fight 'em."

If those conversations were happening outside the walls of

Mt. San Rafael Hospital, they were happening inside as well—and for different reasons. Mary Lee Biber, Biber's fifth and final wife, had worked as a nurse with Biber for more than four decades before marrying him in the final years of his life. She watched as he trained Bowers to take over the ob-gyn and gender confirmation surgery parts of his practice, and she says she could sense trouble coming. Her concerns about Bowers had less to do with the surgeon's impressive medical skills than with her personal style.

For example, when Bowers and her former boyfriend went out to dinner with Biber and his then girlfriend Mary Lee shortly after moving to Trinidad, Mary Lee—at the time working as the quality director at the hospital—says Bowers got off on the wrong foot. "I was like nobody to her," Mary Lee Biber recalls. "She told Dr. Biber, 'We have to find you somebody you can date and have a life with.' And I'm sitting right there. And the guy with her said, 'Marci, that's her. That's his girlfriend.' I mean, it's like, who did she think I was?"

Mary Lee Biber came home from having Christmas dinner with her daughter and heard music coming from her husband's beloved baby grand piano. She'd brought him leftovers and had taken them into the kitchen. She stood by the counter there and just listened for a while. The music was, as usual, beautiful. When she entered the room, and after he finished playing, he closed the piano's keyboard cover and said, "OK, hon, I'm done now."

Mary Lee pauses in telling the story, then says she thinks he knew then that he was dying.

Biber had been diagnosed with pneumonia on December 12 and his doctors had put him on a daily dose of antibiotics. But he didn't improve. About ten days later, he visited a pulmonologist. His lungs sounded clear enough, but the pulmonologist scheduled a biopsy for December 27, two days after Christmas. Biber looked at his doctor. "I don't think I'll make it until then," he said.

The pulmonologist dismissed his concern, saying, "Just go home and take the oral antibiotics and you'll be fine." But Mary Lee Biber says her husband didn't look good.

The day after Biber's melancholy solo Christmas concert, Mary Lee was working at Mt. San Rafael when he called her. She recalls him sounding weak, suggesting that she come home. He'd almost passed out and felt he needed to go to the hospital. She drove home, and then drove him back to the hospital emergency room. An X-ray there revealed a cloudy white mass in one lung and he was ordered to Pueblo for a specialist's opinion. Mary Lee bundled him into the car, along with supplemental oxygen, and drove him there after he declined an ambulance.

Biber was admitted immediately to the hospital in Pueblo, and by that evening he was having trouble breathing. Earlier in the day, when it was clear his health was failing fast, Mary Lee—knowing he'd left a written "Do Not Resuscitate" order—asked him what he wanted her to do if things continued to get worse. He told her he wasn't yet ready to die and asked her to do everything she could to keep him alive. So she and the specialist agreed to place the fabled surgeon on a respirator.

During the three weeks he remained on the breathing apparatus, Mary Lee says she could see the white cloud in X-rays of his lungs spreading, "to the point where both lungs were completely whited out." By mid-January, the pulmonologist was telling her, "Mary Lee, you've got to let him go."

. Biber's fifth wife notified all of Biber's children and urged them to come to Trinidad. And they did. She says she and her husband's doctor agreed to turn off the respirator on January 16, 2006, only after the last two of his nine children and stepchildren arrived and had a chance to say goodbye.

. Following Stanley Biber's death, the bright spotlight on Mt. San Rafael Hospital and Dr. Marci Bowers began to intensify. Biber had never shied away from publicity; Mary Lee remembers the time he allowed Geraldo Rivera and his film crew into the operating room. But the more frequent presence of reporters, photographers, and film crews invited by Bowers began testing the patience of staff members and the hospital board. A June 2007 profile of Bowers in *The Denver Post* about eighteen months after Biber's death was headlined: "Trinidad's transgender rock star."

"Dr. Biber had told Marci, 'Don't flaunt yourself. It's a procedure, not a profession,'" Mary Lee recalls.

Biber's widow recalls journalists from media organizations arriving unexpectedly on the day of a surgery, expecting to be allowed into the surgical wing and the operating rooms. "These are patients who are sick. These are patients' families. Yes, the transgender patients, if they agreed to it, that was OK. But they couldn't just walk around flashing flashbulbs or whatever. And the board called her on it…. All she had to do was just follow the rules. And the rules were not that bad."

Hospital spokesperson Kim Lucero echoes Mary Lee Biber's version of the parting. "It was pretty tense," she says. "Dr. Bowers wasn't happy about it by any means." Asked if she thought Bowers would have stayed if the media access issue hadn't been a problem, Lucero says: "If she could have gotten her way and done whatever she wanted to, absolutely. That's usually with any physician, not just her specifically."

By the fall of 2010, tensions between Bowers and Mt. San Rafael administrators had degraded the point that Bowers was butting heads with an influential hospital board member and the hospital's CEO. "They told her she could continue doing surgery there, but she had to follow some guidelines," Mary Lee Biber recalls. "Marci said she could go to San Francisco and do anything she wanted to do."

———————

Unique is a tragically overused word, but it's accurate when discussing Bowers's perspective when it comes to transgenderism and issues of gender dysphoria. Her insights into trying to address those issues with hormonal therapy and surgery ring with convictions born of deep experience. She not only has for years walked her patients through the late stages of their transition, but she has done so having walked that same road herself.

"I've lived and breathed this process, and even though my day-to-day interactions are as a woman, I'm not out," she says. "I'm a somewhat public figure, but when I go around in the world I'm just like any other woman. Other people haven't been confronted, and they haven't fought so deeply through sleepless nights, or been on call or in the midst of surgery where I can think about these things all day long. That isn't to elevate my status, but I've really, really been there."

Having your hands inside another human being's body, coaxing their unborn babies into the world or burrowing deep inside a mother to retrieve a placenta after birth, or holding someone's vital, pulsing organs in your gloved hands is profound in and of itself. But Bowers says, "when you've taken a magnificent penis and you've stripped it down to its primordial components, it gives you a lot of perspective if nothing else."

As a result, the surgeon tends to be remarkably candid about a lot of things. For example, she knows her thoughts about the inability of non-trans members of the LGBTQ community to understand the transgender journey might alienate some, but she offers them anyway. "Most people in the LGBTQ community don't get transgender men and women. I hope that doesn't get me in trouble, but I do believe that, fully." It has helped that in recent years trans people have been included beneath the community's wide umbrella, she says, because "the your-cause-is-my-cause, your-struggle-is-my-struggle thing has been unifying. But if you come down to the actual points about being trans, they don't get it. But again, it's because they themselves aren't comfortable defending the process."

She's even more blunt about people such as Walt Heyer, who in her more charitable comments she calls a "tragic figure." She points out that he has no training in biology and practices a faith that sees evolution as little more than an annoying theory that contradicts its holy scriptures. She puts little stock in his claim that most trans people who undergo surgery eventually regret it. "This surgery has the lowest regret of any surgery imaginable, including cataract surgery, gallbladder surgery, tubal ligation, hysterectomy," she says. "There's no surgery that has less regret than this one."

Various studies back up her claim, placing post-op regrets at between one and four percent of patients. And when Bowers underscores her point, it's clear she's speaking from personal experience. Patients who opt for surgery so seldom regret their decision because "they've spent their whole life living a lie. By the time they actually go through it they're like, 'Finally! I've already done that. I've already played that game. I've already been the round peg in the square hole. I've done that life. Am I going back to that life? Never. Neh-ver.'"

As for Heyer, Bowers doesn't believe he really understands that the transgender experience is inseparable from human evolutionary biology. The gender spectrum "is part of the complexity of humanity. Nowhere else in nature are choices limited to two, besides gender. It's not sound thinking, biologically, to have just two choices. Logic would say there's a spectrum, and that's probably the arc that we're on. Maybe someday it won't require surgery. Maybe we'll someday be OK with a woman with a penis or a man with a vagina."

She also groups Heyer with others she has known who look at doctors and surgeons as all-powerful and godlike when, she says, they're just skilled professionals who can execute what the patient wants based on accepted WPATH protocols. But what the patient wants—the choices they've made before they ever arrive at the surgeon's office—is critical. Patients are solely responsible for those choices, but sometimes want to blame their doctors when they're disappointed or things don't turn out the way they'd hoped.

As she speaks, for example, Bowers says she is dealing with a young female-to-male trans patient who she says takes an incredibly passive view of his medical providers—an approach that allows him to magnify some of his problems out of proportion. "He says, 'They should have seen this. They should have known this. They should have done this.' It's just one complication after another."

The problem extends far beyond transgender medicine,

she says. "There are people that take a passive role to health care, thinking that doctors are gods and know everything and the choices they make are very black and white. And they just really aren't. So anytime I take a patient to surgery, I just tell them 'I'm just enabling you. I'm not making your decisions for you. I'm your agent of change. I will get you there, but I'm not going to be your protector. I'm not going to be your best friend.'"

Bowers says she became familiar with that issue while in Trinidad when some patients, relieved to find an understanding and compassionate surgeon, expected more of the relationship than Bowers was prepared to give. "The next thing you know, they're bringing minestrone soup and think they want to picnic with me and be my best friend," she says. "Basically, we're the Uber drivers of medical care. We'll get them to their destination, but we're not there to make their minds up, we're not there to steer them clear of danger when they get there. We're not there to entertain them once they arrive at their destination. We get them from Point A to Point B."

Bowers urges those considering gender confirmation surgery to take their responsibility in that decision seriously, rather than relying on doctors for guidance. So many consequences are wrapped up in that single decision—including the chance to have children in the future, or in the case of transgender children themselves, the effects of hormone treatments that may forestall puberty and prevent them from ever experiencing sexual release—that each potential consequence must be carefully weighed. Bowers says she often talks to her patients, especially the younger ones, about those choices before even considering surgery. In those cases, "now suddenly we're grappling with the fact that they don't have enough skin for surgery, so we have to find new sources of skin. And some of these kids, because they've been [hormonally] blocked before puberty, have never before experienced an orgasm. How do you give them a surgery that comes with the risk of nerve damage, or never orgasming? Whose fault is that? The doctor that does the surgery? Shouldn't that sexual thing maybe have been explored a little more beforehand?"

She believes the transgender health experts at WPATH still

have a long way to go in understanding how to factor in the role of sexuality and intimacy when considering surgery for gender dysphoric patients. She recounts a recent discussion with the organizers of an upcoming WPATH seminar scheduled for November 2018 in Buenos Aires, Argentina. "I got two of the leading pediatric endocrinologists to come on a panel with me so we can talk about that," Bowers says of a panel eventually titled "Sexual Function Among Trans Kids with Pubertal Suppression: A Mini Symposium." "Both of them were, 'Yeah, that's a brilliant idea!' And I'm like, 'Why haven't you been talking about this?' Intimacy is a hugely important thing. And if a kid's completely naive to orgasms before they have surgery that could be a real problem."

The debate grinds on. Even an exhaustive, encyclopedic story by Jesse Singal in the July/August 2018 edition of *The Atlantic* about children who say they're trans came to no definitive conclusions about the right way forward: "For some people, it will pass; for others, it can be resolved without medical interventions; for still others, only the most thorough treatment available will relieve immense suffering. We recognize that there is no one-size-fits-all approach to treating anxiety or depression, and a strong case can be made that the same logic should prevail with gender dysphoria.

"The best way to build a system that fails fewer people is to acknowledge the staggering complexity of gender dysphoria—and to acknowledge just how early we are in the process of understanding it."

———

As convinced as she is that Walt Heyer and others who advocate against gender confirmation surgery are wrong, Marci Bowers says she and Heyer do share one thing in common: Belief in a higher power.

"So many people don't believe in God," she says. "And there's so much in religion that drives me crazy. But I actually do [believe], because if there wasn't a higher power, then why are we even here? It makes life kind of futile. And I believe there's something better in the future. What drives me is to figure that out, and to do as much as I can while I'm here to try and do that. It's the most hopeful possibility."

To that end, and in addition to her work with transgender patients, Bowers devotes some of her time each year applying her skills to surgically restoring victims of female genital mutilation. That practice, known as FGM and considered a "purifying" ritual in some cultures, also can have devastating effects on intimacy, relationships, and the health of those who undergo what some call "female circumcision." More than 200 million girls and women alive today have undergone the procedures in thirty countries, particularly in the western, eastern, and northeastern regions of Africa, the Middle East, and Asia.

The World Health Organization condemns the practice in strikingly blunt language:

> WHO strongly urges health professionals not to perform such procedures. FGM is recognized internationally as a violation of the human rights of girls and women. It reflects deep-rooted inequality between the sexes, and constitutes an extreme form of discrimination against women. It is nearly always carried out on minors and is a violation of the rights of children. The practice also violates a person's rights to health, security and physical integrity, the right to be free from torture and cruel, inhuman, or degrading treatment, and the right to life when the procedure results in death ... FGM has no health benefits, and it harms girls and women in many ways.

The least damaging of the four major types of FGM often is referred to as clitoridectomy—the partial or total removal of the clitoris. Restoring those women involves a relatively simple technique that Bowers describes as laying bare the rest of an iceberg whose tip has been severed. In most cases, the surgery lasts less than an hour, but can lead to a lifetime of improved health and happiness.

In 2007 and 2009, she traveled to France to train with Dr. Pierre Foldes who invented the surgical technique that removes scar tissue from the often young victims and exposes what remains of the severed clitoris to restore sexual sensation. She has since done more than 500 such procedures, and between 2017 and 2019 traveled to Kenya to help train local doctors to perform the procedure. Her goal in taking the surgical technique to Africa, she says, was to "allow women to control their own destiny, to regain their sense of identity as women and as sexual human beings."

For Bowers, the move from Trinidad to Burlingame, California, was the right one. She's working on a bigger stage, in a thriving metropolis known for gender diversity. And by improving on the techniques she learned from Stanley Biber, she has established herself in the forefront of surgeons from around the world who specialize in gender confirmation surgery. Life is good, and she looks back on her time in Trinidad as pivotal in her ongoing professional journey. Only after passing through Trinidad did surgeon Marci Bowers become the accomplished professional woman she always believed herself to be.

"I've had a very good run of it," she says, finishing a glass of wine and the last of an elegant Japanese meal. "I found a niche in medicine that few people ever find. I've been a first in some ways. I've been privileged to work with two underserved communities [transgender men and women, and FGM victims]. For me it's been phenomenal."

In an email many months later, though, she looked back on her legacy in Trinidad with a bit less contentment. "I was always considered an outsider. The Porsche and the media will be enduring black marks that the conservatives will hold up as reasons why I was not a true part of Trinidad history in their attempts to dishonor and discredit my legacy there." She instead sees herself "as the linchpin that catapulted Trinidad's role in gender-confirmation surgery into the modern era, allowing for the explosion of transgender icons, growing social acceptance, and surgical programs that have emerged onto the scene today. Mischaracterization of my presence in Trinidad as someone interested in fame and flashy things only echoes the many examples of misogyny that continue to rewrite history as exclusively male in origin."

25

Post-Op Trinidad

You have to search long and hard in Trinidad these days to find any evidence of the diminutive Stanley Biber's once-towering presence here, or even any sign of the town's former stature as "the sex-change capital of the world."

Biber has been dead since 2006. His decades of work, which brought medical pilgrims from around the world, is not commemorated in any way at Mt. San Rafael Hospital where Biber and Marci Bowers performed an estimated six thousand gender surgeries between 1969 and 2010.

You'll find no statue, memorial, or even a plaque marking Biber's long career as the man who brought Trinidad world renown, though many other significant chapters in local history are acknowledged by plaques along downtown sidewalks. It wasn't until May 2019, more than thirteen years after the surgeon's death, that the local museum included any mention of his work in an exhibit space that celebrates practically every other detail of the city's remarkable Old West history.

Until then, the only public evidence that Biber even existed were the personal stories shared by many in town whose lives he touched, and his unremarkable gravestone in one of the local cemeteries.

That's not to say Trinidad is shy about celebrating its history. The Trinidad–Las Animas County Hispanic Chamber of Commerce and the Southern Colorado Coal Miners Memorial & Scholarship Fund Committee commissioned artist Susan Norris to create a statue of a giant caged canary in the center of town commemorating the role those birds played during Trinidad's mining past. It was dedicated on June 4, 2010, and sits not far from the coal miners' memorial by artist Ben Johnson. Dedicated in 1996, Johnson's statue depicts two hard-hatted miners at work loading chunks of coal into a coal car and features the names of dozens of miners who presumably perished in the local mines.

The massive ceramic Trinidad history mural in the lobby of Mt. San Rafael Hospital celebrates three pioneers who "stand out for their contributions to the founding and prosperity of Trinidad," including Dr. Michael Beshoar, Trinidad's first physician, who "organized, guided, informed, and furthered the cultural, intellectual, and political life of the community."

But the mural includes no mention of Biber, who for decades prowled the hospital's halls and whose work once generated a significant portion of its revenue. The hospital once kept a photo of Biber in a special cabinet between two pillars in the lobby, along with some of his awards and memorabilia, but widow Mary Lee Biber says she dismantled it when she moved to Pueblo after his death and turned the items over to one of Biber's closest friends. Mary Lee says she once talked to the city about having a street near the hospital named after her late husband, but says that conversation never went anywhere.

The only hint that Biber spent nearly his entire medical career in Trinidad and brought the town worldwide renown is in the side lobby of the musty First National Bank building on Main Street. Beside the same rickety elevator ridden by thousands of anxious transgender pilgrims is an ancient marble directory listing the building's tenants, including "Dr. S. H. Biber, P.C. Surgeon." It was still there thirteen years after Biber's death simply because no one had bothered to remove it.

"Isn't that interesting," says Mt. San Rafael spokesperson Kim Lucero. "This community does all kinds of recognition, this and that, you just wonder why. It's intriguing, right?"

Lucero wonders if Biber's complicated personal life may help explain the lack of commemoration. Despite having four ex-wives and a widow, and enough children and stepchildren to field a softball team, she points out that there is no single person responsible for or invested in protecting his legacy.

His passage through Trinidad is not left entirely unmarked. Biber is buried beneath a relatively modest granite headstone in a section of the town's Masonic Cemetery reserved for members of

Temple Aaron, the town's only synagogue, where Biber, the former rabbinical student, used to conduct holiday services when no rabbi was available. The Jewish graves are separated from the rest of the cemetery by a low, patchy hedge and an iron entry gate reading "Congregation Aaron." Biber lies just a few paces from the side of that hedge that offers a distant view of Fishers Peak, the distinctive stair-stepped mesa that looms over Trinidad. The front of the headstone reads simply "Biber" in English, with the same name in Hebrew on the back. The front of the stone includes a Star of David centered between the names Stanley H. and Mary Lee, the surgeon's fifth wife and widow who commissioned the stone and plans to someday join her late husband beneath it.

The cemetery grass is still brown, the soil damp, and the partitioning hedge without leaves during an early April visit a dozen years after Biber's death. At the moment it's a lifeless tableau, but with an unspoken promise of spring. Masonic Cemetery Superintendent David Bunce once shoed horses on Biber's ranch in Trinchera, and in addition to Biber he proudly lists a few of the graveyard's other famous or near-famous residents, including British-born Faces bass guitarist Ronnie Lane, who moved from Texas to Trinidad in 1994 and succumbed to complications of multiple sclerosis in June 1997; Louis Tikas, the Greek labor hero and most prominent casualty of the nearby Ludlow Massacre; and one of Kit Carson's daughters.

If you walk twenty paces to the right of Biber's headstone, just outside the Congregation Aaron hedge, you'll discover another headstone that hints at the complicated legacy the surgeon left behind. That's where Ella Mae Biber, his fourth wife, bought a plot in an undeveloped non-Jewish section of the cemetery. Her headstone stands alone and at least twenty yards from any other monuments—but just steps from the gravesite of the man to whom she was married for twenty-three years. She says her intention was to simply be as close as possible to Biber, but it's worth noting that Ella Mae bought the plot and erected the second Biber headstone without mentioning its proximity to Biber's grave to the woman who eventually became his fifth and final wife. Mary Lee Biber was surprised to hear of it.

Trinidad has moved on since Marci Bowers left in 2010, and nothing tangible remains of the city's reputation as a magnet for those grappling with one of humanity's most complicated and misunderstood states of being. The world's transgender pilgrims are no longer "going to Trinidad," or using that euphemism to describe one of the most momentous decisions of their lives.

Following Marci Bowers's departure in 2010, the hospital hired a part-time gynecologist to take over some of the duties she and Biber once performed. No one on the hospital staff is doing gender confirmation surgeries anymore. Mt. San Rafael continues to operate despite dire predictions that, without Biber or Bowers, its revenue would nosedive. Its emergency room sees nearly 9,500 visitors each year, which Lucero says is a lot for a small rural facility. The hospital's average daily patient census is between ten and twelve patients. No one disputes that both Biber and Bowers generated significant revenue for the small hospital, but hospital officials are quick to point out that Biber was a full-service doctor and surgeon in town, rather than a specialist like Bowers. As a result, Biber generated significantly more revenue for the hospital, and his retirement and death likely was far more of a blow than Bowers's decision to leave. Bowers's fondness for Trinidad is apparent, though, in her decision to maintain an insurance and billing office in downtown Trinidad in order to keep several loyal staffers employed. Even so, she seldom visits.

Lately the hospital has been undergoing a $35 million expansion, using federal financing and grants from the Colorado Department of Local Affairs. The upgrades will leave it with a new emergency department and patient-care unit, as well as a new imaging center. When John Tucker, the hospital's current CEO, first began interviewing for the job in early 2015, he had no idea about Biber, Bowers, or the hospital's peculiar history. There was no mention of it in the 2015 Community Health Needs Assessment he read to prep for his interviews. He just knew he wanted to improve access to primary care at the rural hospital for the people of Trinidad and Las Animas County, and says he's proud of the work they've done so far. Clearly, Tucker is looking forward, not back.

The city of Trinidad has moved on as well. Colorado legalized the sale of recreational marijuana on November 6, 2012, and Trinidad quickly became a destination for an entirely different kind of pilgrim. The "green" rush began shortly thereafter, thanks to the city's proximity to the state lines of New Mexico, Oklahoma, Kansas, and the Texas panhandle. Yes, the world's former gender surgery crossroads has transitioned into a center for the legal marijuana trade. By the end of 2018, the city was home to pot enterprises with names such as The Underground Station, The Spot 420-Trinidad, Canna City, and Trinidad's Higher Calling U. The end of town near I-25's Exit 13 looks like a cannabis strip mall, with five dispensaries—Freedom Road, Rooted, Strawberry Fields, Faragosi Farms, and LivWell—lined up practically side by side, right across the street from Michelle Miles's wine and liquor store. *High Times* magazine has nicknamed Trinidad "Weed Town, USA."

Miles, the former Wall Street investment banker who came to Trinidad for gender-confirmation surgery in 2005, bought a home there the following year and moved to the city fulltime in 2010. That was the same year Marci Bowers, her surgeon, moved her practice to California's Bay Area. Miles has been a respected member of the Trinidad City Council since 2012 and has had a ringside seat as the city transformed. With legalization, the city's general fund "flipped" from a dangerous deficit to a surplus. It has attracted thousands of pot tourists, and the town of less than ten thousand residents now boasts more than thirty such enterprises. The revenue is helping with long overdue upgrades to Trinidad's infrastructure.

"I mean, it's not just marijuana taxes that are supporting the town," she says. "My store is a stone's throw from Exit 13. People are getting off and checking out Trinidad. They get off and buy some marijuana, and then they'll look around and say, 'Hey, this is a cool little town. Interesting architecture, mostly nineteenth century. I think I'll stop somewhere for lunch. Maybe we'll stay for the weekend.'"

She says sales and tourism taxes, which had been in decline, are now showing double-digit increases annually. And the city is trying to spend that marijuana revenue wisely, allocating sixty percent of it to upgrade and maintain infrastructure, thirty-five percent to a "rainy-day fund" for sewer main breaks and other unexpected problems, and five percent to promote economic development. She said marijuana-related sales taxes brought in $6.1 million in 2019 and were projected to be about $6.4 million in 2020. "It's pretty healthy. And I can't describe to you how vibrant the downtown feels when the weather is nice. It feels like a city, not a bunch of boarded-up shop fronts."

Still, city leaders already are looking beyond the current green rush because the weed boom may not last forever, especially if neighboring New Mexico legalizes marijuana in the coming years. They envision a community no longer known as the world's sex-change capital, or a place to get legal weed, but as a center for arts and recreation. In 2019, the city and two conservation groups announced a $25 million plan to buy Fishers Peak, the iconic mesa that overlooks the city, as well as the thirty-plus square miles of wilderness around it. They plan to build a hiking trail from the center of town up to the peak, and the site, once developed, will be one of the largest state parks in Colorado.

There's also talk of celebrating Biber, a local '60s-era commune called Drop City, and other creative renegades in a new counterculture museum, which would be part of the new state-driven creative district taking shape in the heart of downtown. In July 2019 it was still in the planning stages, but the possibility suggests a growing acknowledgment of Biber's legacy.

Perhaps the most telling sign that the city is getting more comfortable with Biber's place in local history is the oblique line in the revamped Trinidad Visitor's Guide. Without mentioning Biber by name, it reads: "For half a century, Trinidad welcomed thousands of individuals seeking to become who they were born to be." It touts that as evidence that Trinidad is "one of the most welcoming places in the country."

Trinidad native Jay Cimino, CEO of the Phil Long chain of car dealerships and a benefactor behind a number of town initiatives, also foresees a spot for Biber in the gallery of Trinidad's "champions" he's assembling in the entry hall of the refurbished Champions Building on Commercial Street, not far from Biber's old office. That gallery celebrates not just local sports and education heroes, but also those who "championed" people who needed help. Those include Sister Blandina Segale, a Sister of Charity who helped establish Colorado's first school district in Trinidad and whose kindness is said to have helped convince Billy the Kid to change his outlaw ways.

"It certainly would not surprise me if Biber's name came up as a champion in this town," says Cimino. "It should."

You may have concluded that Biber's obscurity suggests a certain discomfort among locals with his chosen area of specialty, or a continuing marginalization of that important history for transgender Americans. Most locals will tell you you're wrong, including Miles—one of the few medical pilgrims to have made Trinidad her home. She says Trinidad is just not the kind of place that goes around putting up statues and plaques.

"The only commemorations I see are Coal Miners Memorial Park and the Coal Miners Museum, because that's such a rich part of Trinidad's tradition," says Miles. "When it became 'the sex-change capital of the world' people hated that. They really did, because there are such richer traditions. Good lord. Billy the Kid? Bat Masterson? Doc Holliday? It's an incredible history."

Like so much of the West, Miles says, her adopted hometown is "historically driven by people looking for an opportunity to reidentify themselves, and reinvent themselves." Even today, she adds, identity politics don't matter much in Trinidad. "I don't run on trans issues when I run for city council. I just live my life. People casually know that I'm trans, and it's OK, and that's just the way it is."

Paula Manini, former director of the Trinidad History Museum, voiced the same sentiment to NPR in a piece that aired shortly after Biber's death: "You know that Western attitude … what you do is your business, what I do is mine, and that's it."

Dawn DiPrince, chief operating officer of History Colorado, the state historical society, was the lead developer of the "Borderlands" exhibit that opened in May at the Trinidad History Museum. It focuses on how land management and health care changed in that frontier region after the Treaty of Guadalupe Hidalgo moved the Mexican border farther south and made southern Colorado part of the U.S. The exhibit includes a small tribute to Biber—apparently the first of its kind in town—that includes the old camera the surgeon used to take pre-surgery photographs of his transgender patients.

"When you operate in a borderland, you're on the margins, not close to the centers of power," DiPrince says. "If you exist on the margins, there's a lot of opportunity for invention and creativity, and for taking risks that people would not ordinarily do if they were more in the mainstream."

DiPrince says Biber was a perfect example of that, and suggests that remote Trinidad may have been one of the few places where his transgender work could flourish the way it did.

Miles says a more elaborate Biber tribute may someday follow, but notes that the town only recently erected a statue honoring Greek immigrant and labor hero Louis Tikas, the best-known victim in the Ludlow Massacre, and only then because his family and the Denver chapter of the Foundation of Hellenism of America commissioned it. Miles says Trinidad's only involvement was to have city workers build a pedestal along Main Street.

That public commemoration of Tikas took 104 years.

The transgender men and women who once journeyed to Trinidad have found other destinations. Their decisions about where to have surgery are not necessarily based on places, but rather on the surgeons who practice in those places. That was the case with Dr. Georges Burou in Casablanca, Morocco, in the late 1950s, and Biber in Trinidad starting in 1969. Others now travel to see Dr. Pierre Brassard in Montreal, or Dr. Toby Meltzer in Scottsdale, Arizona; or Dr. Eugene Schrang in

Neenah, Wisconsin; turning those similarly unlikely places into transgender crossroads the same way Biber did in Trinidad. There are only so many surgeons who specialize in the procedures, and their locations have made other places around the globe transcontinental magnets for gender confirmation surgery. Some of those places—including Tehran, Havana, Belgrade, and Bangkok—seem no less surprising than Trinidad.

Stryker, the gender historian, sees Trinidad's forty-one-year reign as the world's sex-change capital as a significant link in a chain that these days seems to be getting longer. "I do think the medical tourism angle is really interesting, that you have places where people go to get certain types of work done," she says. "I think Trinidad fits into this longer and broader pattern, like how after the Christine Jorgensen story everybody wanted to go to Scandinavia."

Stryker says Copenhagen ultimately didn't become a Mecca for the surgery because Danes quickly decided they didn't want to become an international center for transgender transformation, eventually limiting the services only to Danish citizens. That decision fueled the rise of Burou's work in Casablanca, just as the demise of big university clinical programs in the US ultimately steered patients to Trinidad.

Now that Biber is gone and his handpicked successor has left town, the Trinidad that once was so welcoming to the world's transgender men and women—a place of more than 6,000 intensely personal transformations—has become a footnote in gender history. The city itself has been transformed, and that particular chapter of its colorful past seems like a distant echo.

Some locals grumble about the city's reputation as a marijuana center the same way many grumbled about its reputation as a transgender medical destination. But from mining to medicine to marijuana to whatever comes next, Trinidad apparently has survived yet another transition. Maybe its failure to celebrate the two surgeons and their patients who brought it worldwide notoriety isn't so much a matter of disrespect as an acknowledgment that the only constant is change, and that transformation is inevitable.

Carol Cometto sits at a table at Tony's Diner, which is located between Trinidad's downtown and Mt. San Rafael Hospital. Its owner, Tony Mattorano, wanders by to say hello to Cometto, and when he realizes that Stanley Biber is the topic of conversation he volunteers two facts: Biber delivered all four of his children, and the surgeon always had a glass of wine when he came in.

He also takes the opportunity to sum up Biber's life in a way that's a little cryptic but says a lot about the legacy Biber left behind: "The Good Book says if you do not sin, you make a liar of God. None of us are perfect."

Whether or not the Bible actually says that is debatable, but Mattorano's fondness for the late surgeon is clear. It's also clear that, memorials or not, the Stanley Biber story lives on in Trinidad locals such as Mattorano, in the babies he delivered, the bones he set, and the lives he touched. His is literally a living legacy that walks and talks and remembers, not just here but in patients from around the world, and it likely will do so for at least another generation.

Bowers's Trinidad legacy may be less entrenched because her time here was much shorter, and the lives she most impacted tended to come and go. But it's alive as well. Cometto, in particular, still misses her former lover, who called her "Lovey," and thinks of Bowers every time she glimpses in a mirror at the "Marci and Lovey" tattoo on own backside. She pulls up the sleeve of her sweatshirt to show off another tattoo on her right bicep, which includes the logo of Bowers's gynecological and surgical practice and the song lyric "Ain't no sunshine when she's gone."

And maybe Bowers's legacy is most alive in her long-range, evolutionary view of transgender and intersex realities as a biological inevitability. That convincing science hovers over the fascinating and complicated history of this obscure Colorado town like smoke from a fire that no longer burns there. As the surgeon says, there may yet come a day when the fleshy apparatuses of genitalia simply don't matter as much as they do right now in a culture that's struggling to make sense of what a June 2014 *Time* magazine cover labeled "The Transgender Tipping Point." But nature doesn't wait for anyone's approval.

Afterword

Martin J. Smith's *Going to Trinidad*, while beautifully written and well-researched, focuses narrowly on two individuals whose experiences may cast doubt on the validity and accuracy of the gender transition process. The described characters are atypical, expressing an unusual degree of uncertainty in their respective gender transitions compared to most who transition, and the many who "go to Trinidad."

The book also gives credence to the viewpoint of Paul McHugh, the notorious Johns Hopkins psychiatrist whose 1979 junk science drove transgender medicine from academic centers into obscure treatment locales such as Trinidad, Colorado; Scottsdale, Arizona; and Neenah, Wisconsin. It also highlights notable transgender diagnostic tragedies. As a result, readers might conclude that those who are resolute in completing the gender transition process strike a Faustian bargain, bartering one's biological origins for some sort of artificial reality—with cancerous consequences for each.

Make no mistake, both of the central characters in *Going to Trinidad* are unusual. However, I feel it's important to acknowledge each story for what it is rather than discount the unusual messaging implied by each subject's journey. I also want to offer a more global and expansive look at what the transgender process is about and where we are all going as we seek happiness and fulfillment in our respective lives—transgender, cisgender, or anything in between.

I understand the fear and misunderstandings about this topic among many who are unfamiliar with our biology. The fact is human males and females share 99.7 percent of the same DNA.

Men *naturally* possess breast tissue, estrogen, emotions, anxiety, and genitalia that are responsible for the development of female anatomical structures. So, too, women *naturally* have measurable testosterone in their blood, and clitorises that can be thought of as tiny penises—some actually not so tiny.

Making things even more complicated, one in 2,000 babies are born with genitalia that are not strictly male and not strictly female, called intersex. That translates to 15,500 intersex persons born during 2020 in the United States alone. Biological diversity leaves them with genitals that are somewhere in between; after all, genitals in both sexes arise from identical embryologic tissues. Their development is complex and not always complete, often hidden until surgically "corrected" to fit a binary anatomical model. But that's changing. Intersex individuals with "imperfect" genitalia have begun to ask doctors and parents to suspend irreversible genital surgery until it can be done with full consent once the child has established a clear gender identity.

Intersex individuals and conditions have existed on earth since creation. So, too, has persisted the desire to change one's anatomical sex to match one's internal feelings. But those countless millions born with intersex, ambiguous, or unusual genitals proved vexing to the rules and mores of ancient societies. Clothing obscures this uncomfortable reality, hiding the in-between genitalia from plain sight. Portrayals of intersex and transgender individuals have varied throughout history, not in their incidence but in their acceptance within society. They appear in mythology, in literature, in the Bible, in traditions, in art—often reverentially credited with having a spiritual balance that their duality brings to judgment and fairness and empathy and kindness.

Eunuchs, for example, are mentioned fifty-nine times in the Bible. Those willingly castrated males feminize in the absence of testosterone, and often were placed in positions of power and leadership because their judgment was felt to transcend the aggressiveness of uncastrated males. Modern Christianity later abandoned the creation of eunuchs and began to confine and constrict definitions of gender into two distinct and wholly separate entities, male and female. In its zeal for perfection, modern Christianity held little room for the ambivalent or the in-between.

But that marginalizes those of us whose own sense of masculinity or femininity does not match the gender assignment made at birth, which usually is the result of a superficial glance between the legs to determine the presence or absence of an external penis. As a result, we are each effectively placed at birth into societal gender cages for which the keys are thrown away. Given the role that maternal hormones, genetics, and the environment play on the development of the complex brain, the internal guidepost of gender identity surely is not universally consistent or limited to just two choices. That people are caged within these gender boxes is not only cruel, but unnatural.

———————

The struggle that Walt Heyer exhibits in *Going to Trinidad* is tragic, without question—although seemingly with a quasi-cheerful, cisgender ending. In his narrative, he unfortunately impugns the process of counseling, diagnosis, and treatment while failing to question the roles of personal decision-making, autonomy, and self-determination. He implies that medical professionals hold ultimate responsibility for his confusing and seemingly illogical series of life choices, which were complicated by substance abuse and mental health issues. Very few individuals anywhere in the world are so ambivalent and transitory in their sense of gender identity, although he appears to have found happiness in denying he was ever transgender.

Claudine Griggs, this book's other central subject, also seems also to have found happiness—but with compromise and a sense that her transition was less than fulfilling. Never feeling quite like a woman, left with physical compromises, she seems to sigh and say, "Oh well." I'll leave for readers to discern whether that was her intent or simply my interpretation of her story.

In both cases, their gender-confirming surgeries in Trinidad were long, long ago (1991 and 1983 respectively). Surgery and society have come a long way since those latter days of the last century, and we've developed techniques that improve realism and sensitivity. That Dr. Biber and other doctors of that epoch were legendary as great surgeons belies the fact that the completed surgeries of their era were relatively rudimentary. The transition stories of Heyer and Griggs may reflect those more primitive results.

Similarly, society as a whole has made progress regarding gender and sexuality. Conservatism and religion sometimes obstruct progress and obscure the diversity demanded by nature, which allows biological spectrums rather than dividing things into neat either/or binaries. No single factor has led to the suicides of LGBT persons more than organized religion, enabling as it has those who extend that intolerance through bullying, mistreatment, denial, oppression, violence, exclusion, and hatred. It causes families to turn their backs on their children, and encourages employers to fire otherwise capable employees. Fascists and dictators, too, use conformity to suppress free will and create soldiers and armies that kill.

Rather than demonizing LGBT emergence as a "gay" or "transgender" agenda, a truly free society will continue to expand and blur the distinctions between male and female. Going forward, it's imperative that in our ideals and our allegiance to God or another power we finally find the one WWJD ingredient that unifies, soothes, and ultimately will prevail—unconditional love. And the face of that love will be neither male nor female.

Trinidad has and always will hold a cherished place in my heart. It is a deeply soulful and enormously beautiful town. I met and befriended many and varied people in Trinidad, and I miss them dearly. I grew tremendously in my professional journey there, and

I'm confident that I left behind a legacy of both hospital profitability and medical progress. I performed five surgeries each week with no access to an intensive-care unit, which Mt. San Rafael Hospital closed in 2004 for budgetary reasons. For years I was the only surgical specialist in that part of the state, caring, as Dr. Biber had done, for anyone who walked in or asked for treatment. I also delivered babies during my first three years there, sharing call with three family physicians and serving as their emergency backup until the hospital closed its obstetrical unit.

At the same time, I took advantage of opportunities to educate the public about the lives of transgender persons in the US and around the world. I continued a tradition begun by Dr. Biber, who allowed Geraldo Rivera's cameras to follow him into the operating room and tolerated the helicopters that circled above Trinidad for days amid rumors that Michael Jackson had been admitted for "sex change" surgery. But the rise in cable television during my era opened the door for lengthier, more graphic, and more realistic portrayals of gender-confirmation surgery. Media inquiries poured in because of Dr. Biber's history and because in 2003 I brought new energy to a place with a magical history. I welcomed the chance to tell our stories.

Word spreads quickly in a town the size of Trinidad. If there was one failure I own, it was my inability to get ahead of rumors and misinformation. Long hours in the operating room left little time for containing any sort of messaging or polishing my charisma. I did my best, but it was exhausting and overwhelming. Most of the community was supportive and enthusiastic about my presence, but after Dr. Biber's death in 2006 some in Trinidad began to undermine the foundations of my efforts there. Dr. Biber left incredibly large shoes to fill. That I managed to do so at all in the face of unspoken opposition is, in retrospect, amazing.

I was not happy to leave Trinidad. I had come to love the town despite the difficulties its remote location created. The airport in

Colorado Springs was two hours away through mountain highways, so travel to conferences and speaking engagements was difficult, especially in winter. Patients who flew into Denver had to make the nearly 200-mile trip to Trinidad. My family continued to live on the west coast, and I missed them.

Plus, many of the pillars of my success began to weaken shortly after Doc Biber's passing in 2006—employees and physicians fired, threats of fee increases, media access to educational efforts diminished. Carol Cometto, my partner during much of my time in Trinidad, had opened a magnificent recovery facility in town, offering quality care for the patients that we loved. But I still felt marginalized in many ways.

Ten years later, more than half of the 2,050 vaginoplasties I've performed have been done at my new practice in California. I'm within reach of Dr. Biber's legendary record of surgeries. The World Professional Association for Transgender Health, which elected Walt Heyer's therapist Paul Walker as its first president in 1979, is turning forty-one years old in this odd year of 2020. Its membership has exploded to more than 2,500 professionals in forty-nine countries. As of this writing, I am now WPATH's president-elect.

For all of us, life is a series of choices and compromises. We make the most of each. Transgender life might never be an easy journey, but like the flowers that bloom each spring, the transgender movement isn't going anywhere, nor are the lessons to be learned from it. The experience of living a life with breadth, multiplicity, and intrigue can be both electrifying and unifying.

—Marci Bowers, MD
November 2, 2020

Acknowledgments

My efforts to reconstruct the pre- and post-op thoughts and experiences of Claudine Griggs and Walt Heyer were simplified by the detailed autobiographies they wrote recounting what they went through before and after their surgeries in Trinidad. If my recap of those experiences mirror their own accounts, it's because Griggs's 2004 *Journal of a Sex Change: Passage Through Trinidad* and Heyer's 2015 *A Transgender's Faith* are remarkable documents in and of themselves. I thank them both for their honesty, their recall, and their willingness to share their most intimate thoughts, fears, and ambitions. Their clarifications and elaborations during our subsequent interviews proved invaluable.

The family of Dr. Stanley Biber helped me reconstruct details of the surgeon's remarkable life, particularly Ella Mae Biber and Mary Lee Biber and several of the children from that complicated family. I only wish I'd had the pleasure of meeting that fine and compassionate surgeon. Dr. Marci Bowers was generous with her time and honest in her personal and professional recollections, as was gender historian Susan Stryker of the University of Arizona. Both were particularly encouraging about this project, and I appreciate their confidence.

A note about pronoun conventions: Sharp-eyed readers will notice that references to Claudine Griggs through this book refer to her using female pronouns. I made that choice because it's both her ongoing preference and fits with her unwavering vision of herself as a woman. In the case of Walt Heyer, the situation was complicated by his own gender confusion, mental illness, and experiences. I used male pronouns when referencing him in the lead-up to his gender confirmation surgery from male to female. During the years he lived off and on as a woman named

Laura Jensen, I used pronouns that best suited his life at the time. But in contemporary references and in instances during which he was transitioning back to a male identity, I used male pronouns, as is his preference.

During the earliest phase of reporting this book, I created a Kickstarter campaign to help fund some of the travel I needed to do. Thanks to those who showed early faith in both the story idea, and me. Some contributed anonymously to a fundraising effort that ultimately failed, but the known backers were: Scott Martelle, Dan Nolan and Merilyn Hunter, Patrick J. Kiger, Kim Christensen, Candice Reed, Alicia Nieva-Woodgate, Rudy Wann, Peter Ralph, Judy Watts, Kurt D. Hamman, Marrie K. Stone, and Jared Polis, who a few months later was elected governor of Colorado. In addition, Brian Golden Davis helped create the video that was part of that campaign.

While doing research in Trinidad, I was given guided tours of the city by lifelong residents Carol Cometto and Dick Hamman, as well as Cy Michaels. Kim Lucero was an able spokesperson for Mt. San Rafael Hospital, and Tom Potter at the Trinidad Carnegie Public Library opened up the history room and steered me to all sorts of interesting material about Stanley Biber. Michelle Miles and her German shepherds, Gus and Jenna, were gracious hosts during a summer 2019 visit and enormously helpful with understanding modern Trinidad. Mayor Phil Rico and City Manager Greg Sund also helped me better understand their city. Dawn DiPrince of History Colorado helped put Biber's work into historical context, and Kirby Stokes and Matthew Trujillo of the Trinidad History Museum were generous with their insights and time. Trinidad native Jay Cimino, one of the country's most successful auto dealers and perhaps Trinidad's most generous benefactor, clearly understands the meaning of "home" and has demonstrated again and again his loyalty to his hometown. Marsha Botzer, founder of the Ingersoll Gender Center in Seattle, helped shed light on her many decades of work with Biber, as well as her role in connecting Biber and Bowers. She also was one of the earliest readers of the book.

Alice Short gave my postmortem profile of Biber and his Trinidad legacy a home on the front page of the *Los Angeles Times*, which led to new sources and opportunities for the book manuscript. I'll forever be grateful for her support and friendship.

I salute the faith that publishers Derek Lawrence, Margaret McCullough, and Caleb Seeling of Denver's Bower House showed in this manuscript, and their recognition that this seemingly local story has far more global importance. Thanks, too, to the members of the Grand County (Colorado) Community of Writers for their thoughtful feedback as this manuscript took shape.

My longtime literary agent, Susan Ginsburg of Writers House, showed early confidence in this project, helped me shape it, and stuck with me even when initial feedback from publishers was more skeptical than enthusiastic. I owe her an easier book next time. Her assistant, Catherine Bradshaw, offered early and important feedback.

As always, my wife, Judy Smith, witnessed the birth of this idea not long after we moved to Colorado in 2016 and believed in the project even after it became clear that the road to publication would be difficult. She has quietly encouraged me through ten published books and countless other writing projects, often has been my front-line editor, and has tolerated my inattention during these occasional obsessions for nearly forty years—longer than I ever had a right to expect. She's the partner I needed long before I ever understood that.

—Martin J. Smith

Notes

1. In the US, those clinical guidelines for surgical candidates today are known as the "Standards of Care for the Health of Transsexual, Transgender, and Gender Nonconforming People" from the World Professional Association for Transgender Health, or WPATH. They originally were called the Benjamin Standards of Care, because one of the earliest sets of those guidelines was written by German-American endocrinologist Harry Benjamin, an Alfred Kinsey colleague and one of the first physicians to work with gender dysphoric persons. WPATH originally was founded as The Harry Benjamin International Gender Dysphoria Association.

2. Jorgensen gradually was joined in the American transgender celebrity pantheon by others, including 1970s pro tennis player Renee Richards; LGBTQ activist Marsha P. Johnson; Sonny and Cher offspring Chaz Bono; US Army whistleblower Chelsea Manning; Ines Rau, the first transgender woman, who in 2017 became the first trans model to appear as a *Playboy* playmate; Zeke Smith, a Brooklyn asset manager who was outed as transgender during an episode of *Survivor: Game Changers*; and actress Laverne Cox of the Netflix series *Orange Is the New Black*; and Elliot Page, the Oscar-nominated actor best known for the 2008 film *Juno*, who came out as transgender in December 2020.

3. Tayman's description of Trinidad as "dreary, a room without paint" is among many such characterizations that have offended the city's leaders over the years. Radio commentator Paul Harvey's December 1984 description of the city as "a dilapidated, ramshackle, windswept mining town of 10,000 mostly unemployed Chicanos" didn't go over well either, triggering a letter-writing campaign among offended locals who convinced Harvey to tell "the rest of the story" in a broadcast the following month. That mea culpa included both an apology and gratuitous acknowledgments of the city's "valiantly" maintained homes, its three museums, and its junior college. Said Harvey: "Trinidad has water that doesn't taste, air that doesn't smell. You can walk down the street at any time and people will wave and speak . . . they even dare to smile."

4. Stepdaughter Kelly Biber recalls watching the episode with Biber in the TV room of his ranch house, and says his anger at the parody was not tempered by the enthusiasm of his grandchildren, who she says explained: "You have to be the most famous person in the world if you're on *South Park*!"

5. The Spanish translation of the river that passes through Trinidad may be as good a characterization as any for the transgender experience described by Griggs and many other of Trinidad's medical pilgrims. One account of how the river got its name involves a small band of Spanish soldiers and priests who were "set upon and slain by Indians." Fearing reprisals, the killers decided to throw the bodies into the stream. Because the soldiers and priests died without ever receiving the sacrament of extreme unction, the Catholic version of last rites, they were forbidden entrance into heaven. The stream came to be known as *El Rio de Las Animas Perdidos en Purgatorio*—the River of the Lost Souls in Purgatory.

6. Worth noting: The cavalry soldiers may have arrived with a wee bit of retribution on their minds. Shortly before the brutal pacification of the Utes in Trinidad, the tribe had attacked and presumably destroyed the cavalry's still-under-construction fort.

7. It's impossible to consider that checkered past without wondering about the preponderance of cash-only legal marijuana shops and grow houses that today dot the town of only 8,100 residents.

8. Widow Mary Lee Biber says Biber continued to lift weights during the final years of his life, sometimes hitting the gym five days a week. And nurse anesthetist Bucky Carr recalls Biber's late-life mission to "build muscle" and his persistent requests for Carr to accompany him to the gym.

9. Biber never formally adopted his two stepchildren with Ella Mae Biber, but considered them his own and always referred to having had nine children—seven biological children plus the two stepchildren.

10. Hirschfeld's work ended in the 1930s as fascism spread throughout Germany. According to Susan Stryker's *Transgender History*, Adolf Hitler personally denounced Hirschfeld as "the most dangerous Jew in Germany" and sent him into self-imposed exile. He died in France in 1935, but not before vigilantes ransacked and destroyed his Institute for Sexual Science in Berlin and set ablaze his library of materials on sexual diversity.

11. Griggs refers to herself as transsexual, and I've honored that choice by using it as she does. But it's worth noting that her choice conflicts somewhat with definition offered in the GLAAD Media Reference Guide: "An older term that originated in the medical and psychological communities. Still preferred by some people who have permanently changed—or seek to change—their bodies through medical interventions, including but not limited to hormones and/or surgeries. Unlike *transgender*, *transsexual* is not an umbrella term. Many transgender people do not identify as transsexual and prefer the word *transgender*. It is best to ask which term a person prefers." Griggs says: "I don't often use the term transgender because I think it confuses the matter of a sex change. One does not change gender identity; people seek gender affirmation hormone therapy and surgeries to accommodate a new gender role. When the private experience of gender role is too painful to bear, people can alter their bodies to change 'attributed gender' (how others perceive them), thereby offering a more comfortable experience of gender role in living as a man or a woman and being perceived as a man or woman. Trying to switch gender role without changing attributed gender often meets with internal and external resistance."

12. Subsequent studies have demonstrated the disturbingly high suicide rate among transgender men and women. According to the largest national survey of transgender people, published in 2011 by the National Gay and Lesbian Task Force and the National Center for Transgender Equality, forty-one percent of the more than 6,000 transgender respondents reported attempting suicide, compared to 1.6 percent of the general population. According to a 2014 survey by the UCLA School of Law's Williams Institute, more than a dozen separate surveys of transgender adults in the United States and other countries since 2001 have found lifetime suicide attempts to be reported by twenty-five to forty-three percent of respondents. Those numbers vastly exceed the 4.6 percent of the overall US population who report a lifetime suicide attempt, and are also higher than the ten to twenty percent of lesbian, gay, and bisexual adults who report ever attempting suicide. But the Willams Institute study also urged further research, noting: "Some surveys and clinical studies have found that transgender people are at an elevated risk for suicide attempt during gender transition, while rates of suicide attempts decrease after gender transition."

13. GLAAD defines *gender non-conforming* as "a term used to describe

some people whose gender expression is different from conventional expectations of masculinity and femininity. Please note that not all gender non-conforming people identify as transgender; nor are all transgender people gender non-conforming. . . . Simply being transgender does not make someone gender non-conforming. The term is not a synonym for transgender or transsexual and should only be used if someone self-identifies as gender non-conforming."

14. The GLAAD Media Reference Guide defines *non-binary* or *genderqueer* as "terms used by some people who experience their gender identity and/or gender expression as falling outside the categories of man and woman. They may define their gender as falling somewhere in between man and woman, or they may define it as wholly different from these terms. The term is not a synonym for transgender or transsexual and should only be used if someone self-identifies as non-binary and/or genderqueer."

15. The French surgeon was still using those drawings when he presented a paper on the technique during a symposium on gender dysphoria at Stanford University in February 1973, by which time he'd performed the surgery on an estimated 3,000 patients.

16. This notion has fallen out of favor, according to GLAAD, and many transgender people find that notion offensive. Most prefer to define their sexual orientation relative to their gender identity.

17. The term *queer*, once considered pejorative, is now defined by GLAAD as "an adjective used by some people, particularly younger people, whose sexual orientation is not exclusively heterosexual (e.g., queer person, queer woman). Typically, for those who identify as queer, the terms lesbian, gay, and bisexual are perceived to be too limiting and/or fraught with cultural connotations they feel don't apply to them . . . however, it is not a universally accepted term even within the LGBT community. When Q is seen at the end of LGBT, it typically means queer and, less often, questioning."

18. *Might* being the operative word, since Walt Heyer had always taken a libertarian view of such things, and was not the type of person who looked to the government for protection. "I wanted Honda to keep me on, but my view then and now is that companies should be free to hire and fire whomever they want."

19. The Ulane decision hardly settled the issue. But the Trump Administration's 2017 claim that Title VII provisions did not protect gay

and transgender workers from workplace discrimination was overturned by the US Supreme Court in June 2020, with Justice Neil M. Gorsuch writing for the 6-to-3 majority: "An employer who fires an individual merely for being gay or transgender defies the law." At the time, it was still legal in more than half of states to fire workers for being gay, bisexual, or transgender.

20. Before 2013, the condition often was called Gender Identity Disorder. But that year the American Psychiatric Association released the fifth edition of its *Diagnostic and Statistical Manual of Mental Disorders* (DSM) and, according to GLAAD, "replaced the outdated entry 'Gender Identity Disorder' with 'Gender Dysphoria,' and changed the criteria for diagnosis. The necessity of a psychiatric diagnosis remains controversial, as both psychiatric and medical authorities recommend individualized medical treatment through hormones and/or surgeries to treat gender dysphoria. Some transgender advocates believe the inclusion of gender dysphoria in the DSM is necessary in order to advocate for health insurance that covers the medically necessary treatment recommended for transgender people."

21. The desire among some in the trans community to start a new life after transition, whether surgical or not, is so powerful that those who intentionally or unintentionally refer to a transgender person by their birth name are said to be "deadnaming."

22. Some in the transgender community consider the term *post-op* problematic because not all transgender people can afford surgery or choose to undergo it.

23. One of the challenges in writing about Walt Heyer–Laura Jensen is choosing the appropriate personal pronoun to use as the two personas struggled through that peculiar purgatory. In passages where Heyer lived as Jensen, I used female pronouns. In passages where he lived as Heyer, I used male pronouns. I tried to limit those back-and-forths whenever possible, and apologize for any confusion this may cause among readers.

24. Griggs says a "less sophisticated" member of her extended family once threatened her, claiming she was the devil capable of shape-shifting and performing evil magic.

25. At least in this regard, Claudine Griggs, Walt Heyer, and Marci Bowers all seem to be saying roughly the same thing.

26. Many trans men and women, often older ones, still refer to the surgery using acronyms GLAAD now considers outdated; in this case, Lori references SRS, short for "sex reassignment surgery."

27. While that may have come as a surprise to Arquette, credible scientists and transgender activists have never disputed that hormones, surgery, or clothing have no effect on one's genetic makeup.

28. In offering that theory, Heyer conveniently omits the fact that the second accident occurred at a time when Jenner's transition already was well underway.

Index

Born in Birmingham, Alabama, and raised in Pittsburgh, Pennsylvania, Martin J. Smith began writing professionally while a student at Pennsylvania State University in the late 1970s. His fifteen-year career as a newspaper reporter took him around the world, from the rural poverty of Southwestern Pennsylvania to Nevada's Mustang Ranch bordello; from the riot-torn streets of Los Angeles to the revolutionary streets of Manila; from pre-glasnost Siberia to the then-new frontier of cyberspace.

Since then, Smith has won more than fifty newspaper and magazine writing awards, and his crime novels have been nominated for three of the publishing industry's most prestigious honors: the Edgar Award, the Anthony Award, and the Barry Award. His 2012 nonfiction book, *The Wild Duck Chase*, about the Federal Duck Stamp Contest and the strange and wonderful world of competitive duck painting, inspired Brian Golden Davis's documentary film, *The Million Dollar Duck*, which won both the Jury and Audience awards at the 2016 Slamdance Film Festival, airing multiple times on Animal Planet in September 2016. In 2017, Globe Pequot published *Mr. Las Vegas Has a Bad Knee*, a collection of Smith's essays about the people, places, and peculiarities of the American Southwest where he lived and worked between 1985 and 2016. *The Los Angeles Review of Books* called the collection "compelling and readable," calling Smith "a master of the essay and human interest profile form" and "one of the best nonfiction writers today."

A former senior editor of the *Los Angeles Times Magazine*, Smith was editor-in-chief of *Orange Coast* magazine in Orange County, California, between 2007 and 2016, during which time the Western Publishing Association five times named *Orange*

Coast the best city/metropolitan magazine in the western US, including four consecutive wins between 2013 and 2016.

Smith now lives in Granby, Colorado, where he helped found the Grand County Community of Writers through the local library district, and is vice president of the board of Habitat for Humanity of Grand County. He is a contributing writer for *Stanford Business* magazine and writes a quarterly essay for Denver's *5280* magazine, which the National City & Regional Magazine Association named the best big-city magazine in the US in 2018 and 2020. In March 2019, a collection of Smith's essays made him a finalist for the association's Herb Lipson Award for Column Excellence. His essays also frequently appear in *Adventure Journal*.